Building St Cuthbert's Shrine

Durham Cathedral and the Life of Prior Turgot

Building St Cuthbert's Shrine

Durham Cathedral and the Life of Prior Turgot

— LIONEL GREEN —

EDITED BY PETER HOPKINS

◄ *Durham Cathedral: the cloister, south transept and tower in 1841, from Billings* PLATE XLV.

Sacristy Press

Sacristy Press
PO Box 612, Durham, DH1 9HT

www.sacristy.co.uk

Published in 2013 by Sacristy Press, Durham

Sacristy Limited, registered in England & Wales, number 7565667

British Library Cataloguing-in-Publication Data
A catalogue record for the book is available from the British Library

ISBN 978–1–908381–12–5

Foreword

The importance and interest of Durham lie partly in the medieval cathedral and castle dominating the great incised bend in the river Wear, partly in the richness and originality of that cathedral which preserves so much from the eleventh and twelfth centuries and shows so many innovative features, partly in the extraordinary richness of the surviving manuscripts which have formed part of the cathedral's library for centuries, and partly in the wealth of archives that record how the cathedral, and the cathedral priory which served it, were organised and resourced in the middle ages. But the importance and interest of this extraordinary site lie also in the historical context in which it was created in the Middle Ages, especially in the period following on from the dreadful aftermath of the Norman Conquest with its sequence of rebellion, death, and ravaging of the land, and in the place where the cathedral was built, a rocky, river-girt peninsula in an area which had been marginal to the English kingdom, which lay well within the ambitions of the kings of Scotland, at any rate until the mid-twelfth century, and which had been so devastated by the new Norman kings of England.

Lionel Green's achievement in this book is to focus attention on Turgot, the second prior of Durham Cathedral Priory after its foundation in 1083. Green sees him in several related ways: as the man who was centrally important to the development of Durham Cathedral and who took a leading role in its construction; as a man who bridged the period of the Norman Conquest in the north, originating as he did in pre-Conquest Lincolnshire and going on to lead Durham Cathedral Priory after its foundation by the second post-Conquest bishop of Durham, the Norman William of St-Calais; and as a crucial link between Durham and Scotland with his remarkable relationship with Queen Margaret of Scotland and, with the last stage of his career, as bishop of St Andrews.

In the course of his passionately-made case for Turgot's importance in these respects, Green provides his readers with many materials and references for exploring the influence on Durham of Norway, where Turgot spent part of his early career in an influential position; for the architecture of Durham Cathedral itself, which Green illustrates and discusses effectively and sensitively; for the archaeology of the site, especially the cloisters; for the Anglo-Norman historians of the early twelfth century, especially Symeon of Durham, whose work Green uses to good effect; and for Turgot's own work, especially in relation to Queen Margaret, on which Green focuses particular attention, reproducing a full English translation of Turgot's *Life of St Margaret, Queen of Scotland*. Amongst all this, Green offers short essays giving background information on topics ranging from the development of Christianity in Norway, to the religious Culdees whom Turgot encountered at St Andrews, to the laver (or washing-place) in Durham Cathedral cloister.

There is much here from which even those who know Durham well can learn, but it is presented in a way which the newcomer to these subjects will find accessible. The subjects which Green tackles are difficult and often much-discussed ones, and readers need not agree with everything he writes. But the image he builds of Turgot as a dominating figure in Durham history is a powerful one, and we are in the author's debt for bringing him so vividly to our attention.

It is inevitably a source of sadness that Lionel Green did not live to see this book published, but his family should feel proud to see it now in print. They will surely too feel gratitude, as we all do, to Peter Hopkins for his energy and commitment in editing the book and bringing it to press.

David Rollason
Professor of History, Durham University

Editor's Preface

It was with some trepidation that I took on the task of preparing Lionel's book for publication. The first three chapters and the seventh existed in annotated typescripts, but with several pages of additional manuscript material awaiting incorporation. There were also some background essays, which have been inserted as grey panels within, but distinct from, the narrative. The remaining chapters were in manuscript form, some complete sections, others merely a collection of notes. Much of the latter had to be omitted, but everything relating specifically to Turgot has been incorporated. Fortunately Lionel left lists of books and articles that he had consulted or intended to read, and I was able to work through these. Lionel had access to the London Library collections, antiquarian volumes as well as works of recent scholarship. He would have wished to record his appreciation for all the assistance he received from the staff there. This help has continued in pointing me towards the article on Turgot's mortuary roll and in supplying digital copies of the architectural drawings by R. W. Billings. I am indebted to the staff of Merton Library and Heritage Service who tracked down most of the twentieth-century volumes that I needed via the Inter-Library Loans system, and ordered articles from the British Library. Many of the older volumes that Lionel had used are freely accessible online through Internet Archive, and some are available as print-on-demand facsimile reprints. Judith Goodman kindly borrowed from the London Library those books and journals that had continued to elude me. Thus armed I have been able to check most of the sources that Lionel had identified.

I am grateful to James Sandeman for permission to reproduce Alan Orr Anderson's translation of Turgot's *Life of St Margaret* as an appendix. Rosemary Turner has expertly redrawn several illustrations chosen by Lionel. Fellow-members of Merton Historical Society and Surrey Archaeological Society have assisted with the editorial process—Mary Day, Vivien Ettlinger, Judith Goodman, David Haunton and Denis Turner. Aware that we lacked expertise on Durham, Jennifer Louis offered to pass a draft to her Durham friends Penny and Robin Minney, who in turn passed it to a leading authority on early medieval Durham, Professor David Rollason. We are immensely grateful to Professor Rollason for commenting on two drafts, for offering to write the Foreword, and for negotiating with the Cathedral and World Heritage Site authorities regarding publication. Finally, I would like to thank the Dean, The

Very Reverend Michael Sadgrove, Canon Rosalind Brown, and Vanessa Ward at Durham Cathedral, and Dr Giles Gasper at Durham University, for their assistance and support in publishing this book. But our deepest debt is to Turgot himself, and to his fellow-monk, Symeon of Durham, who recorded Turgot's, and Durham's, story 900 years ago.

Peter Hopkins

Acknowledgments

Lionel Green has written and spoken over the past sixty years about Merton Priory and its daughter houses. In this book he steps back to the roots of Christianity in Britain, from the life of St Cuthbert to the building of Durham Cathedral to house St Cuthbert's remains. Lionel Green was a member of Merton Historical Society from its foundation in 1951 and served as its President from 2006. He was also a Vice President of Surrey Archaeological Society and Chairman of Dorking Museum and Local History Group. Following publication of *A Priory Revealed, using material relating to Merton Priory* in 2005, he turned his attention to Turgot, whom he had discovered in his researches. During the writing of this book, Lionel Green became suddenly ill and died in June 2010. It is therefore with enormous gratitude that we thank Peter Hopkins for taking on the work of bringing the book to completion.

Sheila Green, Jenny Oliphant, Rachel Beckwith
Lionel Green's wife and daughters

Contents

Introduction

Durham Cathedral is widely recognised as an architectural masterpiece. Bishop William of St-Calais (1082–1096) was responsible for its conception and foundation, and bishop Ranulf Flambard (1099–1128) brought it almost to completion. But these two bishops were also important royal officials, though each fell from favour when a new king came to power. Both bishops were absent from Durham for long periods, in Flambard's case for more than six years. Also, there had been a three-year interregnum between the death of Bishop William and the appointment of Bishop Ranulf.

Who had overseen the construction of the cathedral during these times? In 1866 the Revd J. Blunt FSA, writing of St Cuthbert and his patrimony, and the glorious "pile of stones" set up at Durham to house his remains, remarked that "there was a very learned Prior Turgot in those days . . . who . . . seems to have been a man of much taste and energy. He became Bishop of St Andrews eventually, but came back to lay his bones in Durham Chapter House. Most likely it was he who spirited up the monks to get the money and the architects to spend it . . .".[1]

This is the story of Turgot—a man who, after many adventures in his youth, was shipwrecked while returning from Norway and transported to the realms of St Cuthbert, and who became prior of Durham (1087–1109), an unsung enabler who essentially oversaw the construction of this great masterpiece.

Durham Cathedral exists because it was built as a shrine of St Cuthbert, and our story would not be complete without a 'beginning' which recounts the life and death of the saint.

Every event in the story took place because of St Cuthbert, but bound in with this story of the saint is that of Turgot. Its history began long before Turgot was born, and will continue long after the reader of this tale is dead.

◀ *Durham Cathedral: the sanctuary knocker on the north door, from Billings* TITLE PAGE.

▲ *A map showing sites mentioned in this book.*

CHAPTER 1

The Community of St Cuthbert

St Cuthbert

This is the story of Cuthbert as it has come down to us.[1] He was born about AD 635. He kept sheep on the hills near Leader Water, a tributary of the Tweed, now in Scotland, then in the kingdom of Northumbria. In 651 the young shepherd saw a vision of the ascent of the soul of Aidan, bishop of Lindisfarne, and a few days later heard of his death. This made Cuthbert determined to enter a life of prayer, and he joined the nearby abbey of Melrose.[2]

◀ *St Cuthbert's vision of St Aidan's soul being taken to heaven. Drawing by Rosemary Turner, based on Oxford, University College MS 165 folio 18r.*

Melrose Abbey followed customs introduced from Iona, which differed from those of the wider church in a number of ways, the most controversial being the method of calculating the date of Easter. About 658 Abbot Eata and monks from Melrose went to Ripon (*Hrypum*) to assist the bishop in founding a monastery there. Cuthbert became the guestmaster at Ripon and was said to have entertained an angel sent to test his devotion.[3] However, Ripon was a royal foundation and Aldfrith, subking of Deira, favoured the customs practised by the rest of the Western Church. In 661 the king demanded that the Melrose monks either conform to these practices or resign. They were not willing to change their customs and all returned to Melrose.[4] The controversy was finally settled at the Synod of Whitby in 664 and thereafter the Northumbrian Church no longer looked to Iona but to York. Cuthbert seems to have embraced the new customs wholeheartedly, placing the unity of the Christian Church above individual preferences. According to Bede, in later years Cuthbert dissociated himself from those who insisted on keeping to the traditional date of celebrating Easter.[5]

Meanwhile, back at Melrose, Cuthbert humbly submitted himself to the direction of Boisil (Boswell), the prior, who gave him instruction in the scriptures, and set him an example of the holy life. When Boisil declared that he only had a week to live, Cuthbert asked what could be read in seven days and Boisil produced a copy of St

▲ *Scenes from the life of St Cuthbert: His arrival at Melrose (top left), appointment as bishop (top right), departure for Farne (bottom left), and death (bottom right). From Raine* Cuthbert *pp. 17, 26, 28, 32. Based on an illuminated manuscript of Bede's* Life of St Cuthbert *c.1200 (now London, British Library, Yates Thompson MS 26).*

▶ *Holy Island and remains of the church of Lindisfarne, from MacFarlane & Thomson I p. 153: "From Turner's England and Wales".*

John's gospel in seven parts. They read, discussed and meditated on a part each day until Boisil died on 23 February 662. Cuthbert succeeded him as prior in 664.

Cuthbert was appointed abbot of Lindisfarne in 676 but, after several years in this role, he sailed on to the island of Inner Farne to become a hermit, walling himself in so that during meditations he could see nothing but the sky. His life of solitude ended in 684 when he was appointed bishop of Lindisfarne, after Bishop Eata moved to Hexham. Cuthbert was consecrated on 26 March 685 at York and spent two years travelling the length and breadth of his diocese ministering and preaching. When he realised that his death was imminent he returned to Inner Farne, where he died on 20 March 687. His last request was that, if the monks were ever to leave the island, they would take his bones with them.[6] Cuthbert became famous as a reputed worker of miracles, and both he and Boisil were declared saints.

Cuthbert's body was taken into St Peter's Church, Lindisfarne, for burial in a stone sarcophagus on the right-hand side of the altar.

On 20 March 698 Bishop Eadberht of Lindisfarne gave permission to open the grave for Cuthbert's first translation, which involved the repositioning of the tomb above ground, on the floor of the sanctuary.[7] This revealed his body to be unchanged and incorrupt. The saint was placed in a wooden coffin engraved with angels and apostles, together with a gold and garnet cross, a copy of St John's gospel and other items.[8] In 737 Ceolwulf, king of Northumbria from 729, entered the abbey as a monk, and on his death on 15 January 764, he too was declared a saint.

Post mortem journeys

The area around Lindisfarne was ravaged by the Danes on 7 June 793.[9] The monastery was sacked, many monks were killed, and gold and silver was seized.[10] Following the growing number of Danish attacks between 820 and 830, Bishop Ecgred (Egfrith) of Lindisfarne (830–845) built a church at Norham upon Tweed, dedicating it in honour of St Peter, St Cuthbert and St Ceolwulf. Here were placed the remains of Ceolwulf and, according to some sources, of Cuthbert as well, his shrine perhaps remaining at Norham for about twenty-five years before being returned to Lindisfarne.[11]

Having captured York in 866/7 the Danes began to settle rather than pillage. They set up petty kingdoms, and even appointed an archbishop of York, Wulfhere.[12] The Danish leader Halfdan arrived in 875 to attack Northumbria, and Bishop Eardwulf of Lindisfarne decided to abandon the monastery. The monks removed the body of Cuthbert and wandered for seven (or nine) years, "flying before the face of the barbarians from place to place".[13] With the body they carried the head of St Oswald, the bones of St Aidan and illuminated manuscripts, including the Lindisfarne Gospels. The porters included Hunred, Stitheard, Edmund and Franco. On their journeys they must have encountered all weathers in all seasons—all endured as an expression of their loyalty and devotion to St Cuthbert.

The patrimony of St Cuthbert had been built up from the late seventh century when in 685 King Ecgfrith gave the Carlisle estates to Lindisfarne and the church there dedicated to St Cuthbert. All gifts were held in common by the hereditary families of the community, with St Cuthbert being the one permanent member. In the wanderings of the community between 875 and 883, it was the possession of the saint's body that gave corporeal title to the estates. They preserved their integrity and even enhanced the importance of the community.

Gifts included many estates lying between the rivers Tyne and Tees and some in Lothian. Here the community operated an ecclesiastical franchise and, with it, political influence. The people in the area did not consider themselves English or Scots or even Northumbrians—they were the *Haliwerfolc*—the people of the saint. The quasi-monastic group became known as the *congregatio sancti Cuthberti*. The *congregatio* (community) consisted of a dean and seven clerks who, with their families, held the land of St Cuthbert. One of their number was appointed bishop, and associated with them were priests and secular clerks serving the shrine. Although they did not follow a monastic rule, and did not practise celibacy, they followed the church offices they had used at Lindisfarne.

Their journeys took them to Cumbria, from where they intended to seek safety in Ireland.[14] All "gathered at the mouth of the river which is called Derwent [at Workington]. There a ship was prepared for the crossing, the venerable body of the father was placed on it . . . and they steered the ship on a true course towards Ireland". Suddenly the winds changed and the ship turned on its side, and an ornamented book "fell from it and was carried down to the depths of the sea".[15] Then one man seized the tiller and steered the ship back towards the shore with the wind behind them. They landed safely, but all bewailed the loss of the book.

Cuthbert then appeared in a vision to Hunred, one of the porters, and ordered that, when the tide went out, they should look for the book. The vision presaged that the monk would find a bridle hanging on a tree and that a horse would appear. Several monks went to look for the book and found that the sea had receded much further than normal. After walking three miles or more towards the sea at *Candida casa* (probably Whithorn or possibly Whitehaven), they found the book and discovered "the former beauty of its letters and pages, as if it had not been touched by the water at all".[16] The bridle and horse were found, and used to pull the cart (*carrum*) bearing the saint's body back to Northumbria. The brethren stayed in the minster church of Crayke, 15½ miles (25km) east of Ripon for four months, "as if in their own home".[17]

According to Symeon, St Cuthbert, through a vision to Abbot Eadred, was instrumental in the election of Guthred as the Scandinavian leader and king of York (883–95), bringing a period of tranquillity to the area. The king granted lands between the rivers Tyne and Wear to the *congregatio*, and the saint's body was placed in a church in Chester-le-Street, the episcopal see being moved there from Lindisfarne.[18] Here Cuthbert and the community remained for over a century, protected in part by the defensive perimeter of the Roman fort which still existed.[19] It was also a convenient site from which to administer their estates.

King Athelstan (924–939) made a pilgrimage to St Cuthbert's Church in Chester-le-Street in 934,[20] and gave many gifts, including a gold and ebony cross, a silver chalice, patens, candelabra, four great bells and service books. One treasure was a Gospel Book.[21] King Edmund (939–946) also visited the shrine and made gifts in about 945.[22]

In 995, Aldhun (Ealdhun), bishop of Chester-le-Street, "was forewarned by a heavenly premonition that he should flee as quickly as possible with the incorrupt body . . . to escape the fury of the Vikings whose arrival was imminent".[23] The Danes had sacked Bamburgh Castle in 993.[24] Aldhun left with his monks and journeyed south to Ripon. After a stay of a few months the threat of Danish incursions passed and they decided to return to Chester-le-Street. Soon after approaching the river Wear, the coffin became "so heavie, that all the companie that attended the corps could not draw the waine, whereon it lay; by which they perceived so much of St Cuthbert's minde, that he would not be carried again to Chester".[25] After fasting for three days it was revealed to them that his perpetual place of rest was to be on an uninhabited piece of land at Dunholme (Durham). The site was on a cliff overlooking a loop of the river Wear, "more beholden to nature for fortification, then [*sic*] fertilitie".[26] Here in 995 Bishop Aldhun began clearing the site on the promontory, assisted by Uhtred (Uchtred), earl of Northumbria (*c*.978–1016), and the entire population of the district between the rivers Coquet and Tees. The seventeenth-century writer, Robert Hegge, whose quaint comments are quoted above, remarks that they were "payd for their pains with expectation of treasure in heaven".[27]

Durham Cathedral

Aldhun built a shrine with timber and boughs of trees, after which they built a church of "noble workmanship and by no means small in scale . . . Meanwhile the holy body was translated from that little church (mentioned above) into another which was called the White Church, and there it remained for three years while the larger church was being built".[28] This implies that there were three churches in all.[29] However, the monk Reginald of Durham, who was writing between 1162 and 1173, seems to identify the White Church with the pre-Conquest cathedral.[30] On Sunday 4 September 998 Cuthbert's body was translated into the east end of Aldhun's new cathedral.

The Saxon cathedral

Some idea of the design of the Anglo-Saxon cathedral of 998 can be glimpsed from a record of Ramsey Abbey, Cambridge, which was begun in 969 and dedicated in 974. It had a stone tower, which was rebuilt and rededicated in 991. At the west end was a second tower, which "offered a beautiful sight from afar to those entering the island".[31] Other churches built towards the end of the tenth century include St Mary-de-Castro in Dover Castle, Norton, County Durham, and St Mary, Breamore, Hampshire. Several common features are apparent. Each had a single tower at the west end, typical of the Anglo-Saxon tradition, and a crossing tower with a porticus (subsidiary chamber) on the north, south and east sides, with that on the east narrower than the crossing width; the nave was aisleless and the same width as the crossing. Doorways above the east and west arches of the crossing at Dover suggest a two-storey attachment or spaces in the roof.

The reconstructed plan shown is based on the plan of Breamore, Hampshire. However, a dowsing survey in the cloister at Durham in the 1980s seems to reveal a much larger structure, with a long narrow porticus at the east end, large transepts, and an aisled nave (see plan on p. 58). The west end is more difficult to interpret.[32]

Church towers were unknown before the Danish invasion but became popular in the tenth century. Masons had learnt to overcome problems of towers by the addition of shafts and mouldings, transforming them into works of art. At the angles they used 'long and short' masonry. The central tower became a status symbol, as it could be observed at a distance. It was hazardous for the builder, as it was built on arches above the main body of the church, and stone had to be hoisted high above the ground. Western towers were built at Ramsey (970s) and Brixworth (980s). The upper chamber housed the bells, which were rung from the chamber below, not from the ground floor which was used as a chapel. This became the oratory, with its own altar at the west end, as set out in the *Regularis Concordia* of 973. Bells were an important feature of the time, with tower openings high up as sound apertures.[33]

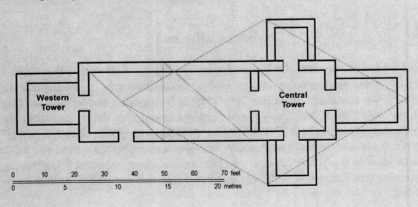

Reginald informs us that "there were two stone towers, as those who have seen them have reported to us, rising high into the air, the one containing the quire, the other indeed standing at the west end of the church; which, being of wonderful magnitude, carried brazen pinnacles [*aerea pinnacula*] erected at the summit; and which exceeded as much the wonder as the capacity to admire of all people. Whence they thought a work of similar structure could be built nowhere else; for the reason that, within the bordering limits of the neighbouring region, all the things necessary in nowise could be brought together in like manner in one place".[34] This refers to the easy supply of stone known as Low Main Post sandstone, which can be cut and sculptured easily and was available from quarries across the river gorge.[35]

At the time of Bishop Aldhun's death in 1018, "he left only the western tower unfinished, and the church was brought to completion and dedicated by his successor", Edmund (1020–42).[36] It was slender, with no buttresses, and no offset courses, and Edmund must have "heightened a western porticus of the tenth-century building to form a tower".[37]

The Danes, who had caused so much devastation in places associated with St Cuthbert, now became worshippers of him in Durham. Cnut (Canute) I, king of Denmark, Norway and England (1016–1035), made a pilgrimage in 1031 by walking barefoot for five miles from Garmondsway[38] to Cuthbert's tomb at Durham, and added to the endowments of the shrine.[39]

Early in 1040 Duncan, king of Scotland (1034–40), besieged Durham, but was unsuccessful and fled in confusion. Many Scotsmen were killed and Duncan was murdered by his own surviving troops.[40] Some say he was killed by Macbeth.

Tostig and Durham

Edward (later known as the Confessor), son of Æthelred, succeeded to the throne of England in 1042, on the death of Cnut's son, Harthacnut. Edward married Edith, daughter of the powerful Earl Godwine of Wessex, and in 1055 appointed Edith's brother, Tostig, as earl of Northumbria. Tostig found the clerks of the *congregatio* at Durham full of resentment as they had had no say in the choice of their bishop.

It had been a long tradition that the community chose their own bishop, usually from one of their number. Some of the clerks were known to be descendants of the original porters of the body of St Cuthbert. This tradition ceased when Bishop Eadred purchased the bishopric from King Harthacnut in 1041. Eadred's successor was a monk named Æthelric, whom Bishop Edmund had brought from Peterborough. The clerks suffered him until 1045, when they rebelled and drove him out of Durham. Siward, earl of Northumbria, intervened and forced the clerks to accept Æthelric. Tostig was appointed earl on the death of Earl Siward. In 1056 Bishop Æthelric resigned, probably because he no longer had Siward to support him. Tostig chose Æthelric's brother, Æthelwine, who had been at Durham for twenty years. To the clerks, Æthelwine was just as unpopular.[41]

◀ *Suggested ground plan of the first Durham Cathedral 998–1092, built by Bishop Aldhun (990–1018), western tower by Bishop Edmund (1020–42).*

Tostig married Judith of Flanders, and both were benefactors of churches, particularly Durham Cathedral, and these were sincere gifts and not deathbed bequests. Both revered the name of St Cuthbert and went to pay their respects, but no woman was allowed to worship at the shrine. Judith sent one of her maids to attempt to do so and a fierce wind blew, which prevented her. She fell and was hurt, and retired to bed, where she died. Tostig and his wife tried to appease Cuthbert and presented to the cathedral a large crucifix, clad in gold and silver and containing figures of St Mary and St John the Evangelist.[42]

In 1060 Ealdred, bishop of Worcester, was appointed as archbishop of York but the pope refused to allow him the pallium of office while he retained the see of Worcester. Tostig and Judith travelled to Rome as pilgrims in 1061 and also to plead for Ealdred. After initial refusals by the pope, Tostig brought him round to a favourable view and won his approval for Ealdred to become the archbishop of York.[43] While Tostig was in Rome, King Malcolm of Scotland, his "sworn brother", chose to attack Lindisfarne.[44]

Tostig also helped his brother Harold fight in Wales in 1063 but was criticised in Northumbria for being away so much. A heavy tax he levied did not assist his case, and Tostig precipitated a revolt in Northumbria in 1064 when he executed three noblemen of the house of Bamburgh, including Cospatric, the youngest son of Earl Uhtred. In March 1065 Alfred Westou, sacrist of the Cuthbert community, exhibited the recently exhumed body of King Oswin of Deira, an early Christian martyr. Many Northumbrians linked the early and recent murders, and Tostig was outlawed and forced into exile in October, and the rebels declared Morcar to be their earl. Tostig and his family left on 1 November 1065, for Flanders and the court of Count Baldwin V, where they spent Christmas.[45]

In November 1065 King Edward fell ill, and on 28 December 1065 his new abbey at Westminster was consecrated. Harold claimed the kingdom even before Edward died on 5 January 1066. Tostig felt aggrieved, and with two of his sons sailed up the east coast of England in April and ravaged Lindsey (the northern part of Lincolnshire). He may have hoped to negotiate with his brother for the return of his earldom, but took refuge with King Malcolm in Scotland. It is possible that Tostig then sought to enlist the help of King Harald Hardrada of Norway to help win back Tostig's old earldom of Northumbria, and enable Hardrada to claim the throne of England as Cnut's successor. Norwegian forces first landed in Scotland and then sailed down the Yorkshire coast, entered the mouth of the Humber, and in September disembarked near Selby. Morcar was defeated at Fulford Gate, south of York, on 20 September. But on the 25th, at Stamford Bridge, Harold of England surprised the invaders, and both Tostig and Harald Hardrada were killed, along with the cream of Norwegian nobility.

Harald's son Olav survived the battle, having been left to watch their ships, and Harold allowed him to take his father's body back to Norway. Two sons of Tostig, Skuli Kongsfostre and Kentil Krok, also survived and went back to Norway where Olav, now king, treated them well. Harold agreed that the survivors could return to Norway in their ships. They had come in 250 ships, but 25 sufficed to take them home. Certain Anglo-Saxon nobility also took ship to Norway, perhaps not wishing to be ruled by a 'West Saxon' king, or possibly anticipating Harold's defeat by the duke of Normandy.

The Norman Conquest

On 14 October 1066 Duke William overcame the English army at Hastings, and began ruthlessly subduing areas of resistance. A Norman, Robert Cumin, was appointed to the earldom of Northumbria, and late in 1068 made his way to Durham, where Bishop Æthelwine (1056–71) invited him to stay. On the night of 27–28 January 1069, the Northumbrians marched to the city and set fire to the bishop's house.[46] Robert and his men were massacred and sparks from the fire were carried dangerously near to the western tower of the cathedral. Prayers to St Cuthbert by the monks were answered with an east wind and the church was spared. The king sent an army north to avenge the massacre but Symeon of Durham relates that at Northallerton his troops were enveloped in thick fog and had to return home.[47]

In September 1069 the Danes landed and sacked York. Cospatric, the new earl of Northumbria, and Edgar the Ætheling[48] decided to join them. William led his army north and dispersed the rebels, but for sixty miles between York and Durham he destroyed villages and monasteries. This was the 'harrying of the North', and Bishop Æthelwine of Durham was apprehensive for the safety of Cuthbert's relics. The community, with wives and children, took up the sacred coffin once more, and departed on Friday 11 December 1069. The first night they stayed at Jarrow, the second at Bedlington, and the third at Tughall, near Bamburgh, until they came once more to Lindisfarne. It was high tide and a cold December night. All were in despair.

"The sea suddenly drew back … and allowed them dry passage across".[49] They remained at Lindisfarne until March 1070, re-entering Durham with praises on 25 March, and laid the saint's body back in its place. But during their absence the cathedral had been plundered. The crucifix, too large for the plunderers to remove, had been thrown down on the ground, severely damaged and stripped of its rich decoration.

▲ *St Cuthbert's shrine passes through divided waters to Lindisfarne when the community flees from William I in 1069. Drawing by Rosemary Turner, based on Oxford, University College MS 165 folio 159r.*

This was the crucifix which had been given to the cathedral by Earl Tostig and his wife. The cathedral was rededicated.

King William returned south in 1070 and rapidly built castles at Lincoln, Huntingdon and Cambridge, garrisoning them to prevent further rebellions. The Danes, together with Edgar the Ætheling, left York, crossed the Humber, and attacked and plundered Lindsey, but were defeated by a Norman force from Lincoln. It is at the castle of Lincoln that our story of Turgot begins.

But first, another glimpse of Norman Durham. Early in 1072 William decided to make Durham a marcher lordship to secure his northern border. He appointed a cleric from Lorraine named Walcher as bishop of Durham, and ordered a castle to be built in the city "where the bishop might keep himself and his people safe from the attacks of assailants".[50] The king then marched north again into Scotland, and on his return called at Durham. King William queried the very existence of the saint, "so he decided to investigate the matter by a visual inspection". He let it be known that if he discovered any imposture, "he would give orders for all the most noble and most senior to be executed. While everyone was in great fear and was imploring the mercy of God through the merits of St Cuthbert, and the bishop was celebrating mass, it being the feast of All Saints, the king wanted to put into effect the idea which he had conceived, when suddenly he began to burn with a terrible heat . . . ". Hastening to leave the church, he forwent the banquet prepared for him, and mounted his horse, "ceaselessly urging it to gallop until he reached the river Tees" and crossed out of Northumbria.[51]

CHAPTER 2

Turgot the Traveller

Turgot of Lincoln

Turgot (also spelt Thurgot, Thurgod or Thorgaut) was born in Lincolnshire about 1048, and came from a Saxon family of good standing, burghers of Lindsey, although the Scandinavian spelling of his name suggests that he was named after the Norse god Thor.[1] The Anglo-Saxon aristocracy ceased to exist after 1066 when many families were effaced. Turgot resided in or near the city of Lincoln and was probably educated at the minster church of St Mary[2] by the secular canons there. It would have been there that he learnt psalmody, the art of singing psalms, which stood him in good stead for the remainder of his life.

Lincolnshire was an important part of the Danelaw, the midland counties of England formerly under Danish occupation. Lincoln was a thriving trading centre, where the sale of wool was the main trade, resulting in the intermingling of Anglo-Saxon culture with Danish and Norse traditions. Lincoln had been the centre of the bishopric of Lindsey from 678 until 958 when it became part of a huge see of Lincoln, but based on Dorchester, Oxfordshire. Later, in 1072, King William the Norman made Lincoln a cathedral city once more.

When Cnut conquered England in 1016, the area was probably treated with greater favour by the Danes. The army was based on shire towns such as Lincoln, whose population in the 1050s would have been about 5,000. There must have been great fear that the prosperous period was over, when William I took over in 1066. England was rich, with a settled government and fair justice. Everyone accepted taxation where the geld was based at a fixed rate on every hide of land. They had a well tried coinage system, but what was to be used in the future?

Rebellions took place, particularly in 1068, and William used his army to quell them. He built castles to dominate the towns, and the citizens of Lincoln witnessed the building of theirs in 1068. The castles required space, which meant the demolition of houses, which in Lincoln amounted to 166 homes.[3] No property was allowed close to the walls of the castle, so surrounding land was also cleared. The building of every castle involved a massive amount of forced labour. When complete, a few hundred troops were able to dominate the population, although they themselves were confined, to live, eat and sleep in a wooden tower built on a motte—an artificial mound. A few local men of some standing were held hostage to guarantee good behaviour for all Lindsey.[4] One of them was Turgot, who was detained in the castle, where his quarters cannot have been better than those of the troops guarding him. His Scandinavian name no doubt prompted the Normans to hold him, fearing an attack from a northern alliance. But by judicious bribery he contrived to escape from Lincoln and make his way to Grimsby.

Turgot in Norway

It was about this time that William I wished to engender friendly relations with Norway. He was conscious of the loss of most of the nobility of Norway at Stamford Bridge in 1066. Envoys were despatched to Norway, and sailed from Grimsby with an unsuspected stowaway. When Turgot was discovered, the Normans asked the Norse crew to turn back, but the request was ignored. Many ties of trade, friendship and speech between the Danelaw and Norway favoured Turgot, and he landed safely in Norway. He soon won the approval of the Norse nobles by his conduct, and was accepted as a Saxon cleric.

When King Olav III heard that a clerk had come from England, he took Turgot for his master in psalmody,[5] making him a member of the royal court. Olav loved splendour and ceremonial pomp, and he also enjoyed comfort—he introduced fireplaces in the walls of his mansions to get rid of smoke-filled rooms. He is believed to have introduced 'guilds', founding the *Miklegild* at Niðaróss, which provided social security and sickness benefit.[6]

The king set about strengthening the power of the Church in Norway, continuing the work of his father. There was no regular diocesan organisation in Norway, and the first bishops were all consecrated in England. When, c.1070, he set up three dioceses he encouraged bishops to reside in the towns to demonstrate the power of the Church in the community, a policy adopted two years later by King William of England. Apparently Turgot assisted with the administration of the dioceses. In 1953 a writer on the Norwegian Church claimed that Turgot "was for many years the King's most trusted adviser . . . to whom the Norwegian Church owed much of its early organization", but he provided no evidence in support of such a statement.[7]

Olav also recalled what his father had recounted about the important buildings in Europe and the Middle East. He resolved to build a large cathedral to enshrine the remains of both his uncle Olav II, who had been declared a saint in 1035, and his father Harald Hardrada. Turgot was involved in planning the construction of the early buildings, and it is likely that this experience influenced his later work in Durham.

Were Durham Cathedral's round piers and classical moulded plinths on broad flat bases modelled on those in early churches in Norway, a style possibly derived from Armenia and Syria?[8] In Niðaróss Cathedral were reeded cylindrical piers, with scalloped capitals. One such pillar has been reconstructed from fragments found in the lapidarium.[9] Was their style copied from similar piers at Durham Cathedral (c.1095), or had Turgot been inspired by them while working in Norway?

Turgot continued to be patronised by the king and amassed a considerable fortune. However, after spending six years with King Olav he began to tire of the pleasantness of secular life (*jocunditas seculi*),[10] and in 1074 decided to return to England.

The Church in Norway

According to some manuscripts of the *Anglo-Saxon Chronicle*, Olav Tryggvason, later Olav I of Norway (995–1000), fought and won the battle of Maldon in 991, after he arrived in Essex with 93 vessels.[11] He became influenced by the Anglo-Saxon Church, and was baptised in the Viking settlement on the Isles of Scilly, by the bishop of Winchester. King Æthelred (968–1016) bought off Olav in 994 with a promise to support his venture to take Christianity to his own country. Neither Sweden nor Denmark had attempted to evangelise Norway, although they had received the faith of Christ by the ninth century.

The sagas record that Olav returned to Norway accompanied by Bishop Jon Sigurd from Ramsey and several priests. They landed at Trondheimfjord in 995, and Olav was declared king. He built a timber church at Niðaróss, and in 997 dedicated it to St Clement, a name he remembered from England. The king attempted to destroy local idols in the Niðaróss (Trondheim) district, and became involved in a power struggle with the chieftains. The ordinary man was content with the new religion into which he was able to integrate his deities and customs, but the result was the presence of many real or pretended Christians. For a time Niðaróss was Norway's capital.

A second Norwegian king called Olav (1016–30) had been converted in 1013 while in Normandy. He wished to consolidate the Church, and all the clergy of Norway were placed under the authority of the archbishop of Bremen. Olav II made new rules for the governance of the Church, and rebuilt the town of Niðaróss and its church of St Clement. Although in 1026 his fleet was victorious in a naval encounter with the Danish and English king Cnut, he lost the support of the Norwegian nobility, who encouraged Cnut's invasion in 1029. Olav had to seek haven in Russia until 1030, when he advanced via Sweden with a small army and reached Stiklestad where he was killed in battle on 29 July 1030. He was regarded as a martyr and his body taken to Niðaróss and buried in a sandbank by the river Nid. A small timber chapel was erected on the site, but his body was later enshrined on or near the altar of the church of St Clement on 3 August 1031. When disinterred, his body was found to be incorrupt. Olav was canonised and accepted as patron saint of Norway.

St Olav's son, Magnus, king of Denmark and Norway (1035–47), moved to Niðaróss in 1042. Every year on 3 August he opened the sarcophagus and trimmed the beard and cut the nails of his father's body.[12] Magnus died in 1047, and was also buried in St Clement's Church.

He was followed by Harald Hardrada (1047–66), who founded the city of Oslo and built its cathedral about 1050, dedicated to St Hallvard. Harald Hardrada had been forced into exile at the age of 15 and served as an army officer from 1034–45, in the service of three Byzantine emperors,[13] at Constantinople, Babylon and Jerusalem. He visited Athens (1040), Sicily and Egypt, and was leader of the Varangian Guard.[14] He returned to Norway with rich Byzantine treasure and a desire to build.

The Northmen of Norway in the eleventh century were at the forefront of building design, with new principles of construction and a new style of building.[15] At Niðaróss he rebuilt in stone the church of St Clement and the Maria church nearby. At both Niðaróss and Selje, the remains of capitals and plinths have been found whose style of mouldings is so unusual as to suggest it derives from churches in Armenia and Syria.[16] After Harald's death at Stamford Bridge his son Olav took the body back to Norway, but contrary winds forced him to winter in Viking Orkney. He finally arrived at Niðaróss in 1067, and Harald Hardrada was buried in the Maria Church which he had built.

Olav III Kyrre ('the Peaceful') (1067–1093) set up dioceses in Norway about 1070, at Niðaróss (St Olav), Oslo (St Hallvard), Bergen (St Sunniva), and probably Stavanger, although there was no cathedral there, only a manorial chapel.[17] The cathedral churches of Niðaróss, Oslo and Bergen were first dedicated to the Holy Trinity, following the example of Canterbury,[18] and all became known as Christchurch, the Church being considered the mystical body of Christ.

At Niðaróss the eastern part of the cathedral was set out in 1071, near the church of St Clement. It consisted of presbytery and transepts, although there were aisles and no eastern chapels in the transepts.[19] The king was able to transfer St Olav's body to the cathedral at its dedication on 30 April 1077. Work on the cathedral continued into the twelfth century. The churches of St Clement and Maria were removed to enable the cathedral to be enlarged.

At Oslo the building of the cathedral began in the late eleventh century with the choir completed by 1130, when the crusader King Sigurd was buried against the north wall.

At Bergen the see was known as Selje-Bergen and the bishop was based on the island of Selje, off the coast of Norway, where a sanctuary to St Sunniva had been set up by King Olav Tryggvason about 996. Sunniva was said to have been the sister of St Alban and daughter of an Irish king, who fled to Norway to escape a heathen prince, and finally died on Selje. Soon after 1067 a relic of St Alban was taken from Ely, England, to the island of Selje, to join the relics of St Sunniva. The first bishop was Bernard. The sanctuary was situated half-way up the cliff on the north-west side of the island, and at the foot was the Benedictine monastery of St Alban. The name of the diocese was changed to Bergen when the relics of Sunniva were taken there on 8 July 1170.

Archbishop Adalbert of Bremen died in 1072, and King Olav withdrew Norway's churches from that jurisdiction. Eventually, in 1103, the bishop of Lund, now in Sweden, was nominated metropolitan, an arrangement which continued until 1152, when Cardinal Nicholas Brakespeare, bishop of Albano, Italy, was sent from Rome to reorganise the Scandinavian Church. The existing cathedrals had no chapters or equivalent staff to sing the daily office. He made Niðaróss the archdiocese on 28 November 1154 to oversee eleven new dioceses, not only in Norway, but Iceland, Greenland, the Faröes, Orkney, Sodor and Man and the Western Isles of Scotland. Bishoprics were to be supported by suffragan bishops.

Country	Dioceses
Norway	Niðaróss, Oslo, Bergen, Stavanger and Hamar
Iceland	Skálholt, Hólar
Greenland	Garðar
Faröe Islands	Kirkjubøur
Orkney	Kirkwall
Sodor & Man	Peel St Germans, including the Western Isles

The diocese at Hamar had been set up after the district was detached from Oslo in 1152. At Niðaróss the Augustinian monastery of Helgeseter was founded around 1170, and the bishop was *ex officio* abbot, with the prior a member of the cathedral chapter.

King Hákon IV (1217–63) transferred the capital in 1223 from Niðaróss to Bergen, and it was removed in 1299 to Oslo. A little before 1483, the bishopric of Niðaróss was renamed Trondheim.

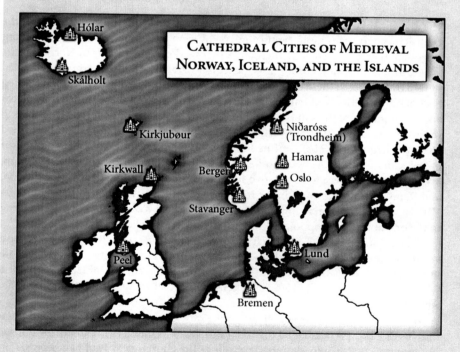

▲ *Cathedral cities of medieval Norway, Iceland and the islands.*

Why would Turgot wish to return to England, knowing that the Normans ruled the country? He may have received news from traders that monasteries in England had not lost their status in society and had been allowed to keep their lands. This was important to him and he felt that he could serve the Church better in a religious community than as an administrator in a foreign land.

He set sail for home, but lost all his property in a shipwreck, only he and six crewmen surviving. Destitute, he made his way to Durham, where Bishop Walcher (1071–1080) listened to his adventures and his desire to become a monk.

The England that Turgot had known was no more, for it had become French. The labourers in the field, woodcutters in the forest, quarrymen and others still spoke in their English dialects, but the king, court, bishops, earls, sheriffs, landowners were now French. In language, dress and society all were French, except that they had become the English.

Refounding the Northumbrian monasteries

The ancient abbeys of Bernicia, later Northumbria, had suffered at the hands of the Danish invaders of the ninth century and many were abandoned. Abandoned, but not forgotten, thanks to Bede's writings and other works by the monks of Northumbria.

Aldwin (Ealdwine), prior of Winchcombe Abbey, Gloucestershire, had been moved by reading of these monasteries in Northumbria, filled with holy men leading lives of mortification and self denial. He resolved to seek out these ruined holy places and, in imitation of the saints of former days, to lead a life of poverty. He wished to restore the traditions of the Northumbrian saints Aidan (died 651), Cuthbert (died 687), Ceolfrith (died 716), and Bede (died 735). No one else at Winchcombe was of the same mind as Aldwin, so he went to the neighbouring abbey at Evesham, Worcestershire, where he found two interested brothers, Elfwy (Ælfwig), a deacon, and Reinfrid, a novice and former Norman knight.[20] Their abbot Æthelwig (1058–77) blessed the three and allowed them to break their vows of 'stability' (remaining in the one house), and appointed Aldwin the superior to keep a strict discipline.[21]

They departed on foot in March 1073, with an ass carrying liturgical books and vestments, and travelled north to Munecaceastre (Monkchester, now Newcastle upon Tyne). A guide through Yorkshire was provided by the sheriff Hugh fitzBaldric who, a few years earlier, had aided the hermit Benedict of Auxerre in founding Selby Abbey.

Walcher, bishop of Durham, heard of the monks' intentions and welcomed them into his diocese. He persuaded them to move from Munecaceastre to Jarrow (Girwa or Gyruum), Bede's ruined monastery, where the church of St Paul had been set on fire by King William's troops in 1069.[22]

Bishop Walcher sent Turgot, "a man still in clerical habit but who was emulating the life of the monks by his love and his deeds . . . to the monastery of Jarrow to live as a clerk among monks under the rule of Aldwin".[23] Turgot soon realised that the Conquest had brought a new vitality and vision into monastic life. At Jarrow some walls still stood, but the buildings were roofless, and the monks covered these with rough timbers and straw, and immediately began divine service. "They made a hut for themselves under the walls, where they might sleep and eat, and they sustained their life of poverty by the alms of the faithful".[24] In 1074 Bishop Walcher assisted the monks and gave them the *vill* of Jarrow with its dependencies. A year later he granted them St Oswin's Church, Tynemouth, in his capacity as earl of Northumbria.[25]

Others joined them, for Aldwin was "sharp of mind, wise in counsel . . . desiring always heavenly things, and inspiring everyone he could to go along with him",[26] and these included Turgot. A few were Northumbrians but most came "from the southern parts of England".[27]

▲ *Church and remains of the monastery at Jarrow, from MacFarlane & Thomson I p. 175: "From Surtees's Durham".*

As numbers increased, Aldwin planned to occupy other deserted monasteries. Thus, in 1075, he left the monastery of Jarrow, leaving Elfwy in charge as prior, while Reinfrid left for Whitby to settle as a hermit among the ruins of St Hild's abbey. Reinfrid had seen the destruction, when he served in the Norman army.[28]

Aldwin, with Turgot as a companion and partner in his plans, travelled to Melrose Abbey, near the Tweed in Scotland, which had belonged to the Cuthbert community but was now abandoned. It was here that St Cuthbert first wore the habit of a monk in 651. They were delighted by the seclusion of this former monastery, where they could live in the service of Christ, and Melrose began to flourish. Cospatric, former earl of Northumbria, who had sought refuge in Scotland in 1073 and had become ill, heard that Aldwin and Turgot were living "in poverty of goods and spirit at Melrose".[29] He summoned them to hear his confession before he died. They were able to offer comfort, and he gave them two ornamental altar hangings. King Malcolm of Scotland also learnt of their presence and demanded their oath of allegiance to him, which they refused. It may have seemed to him that the Normans wished to increase their influence in the north. But Malcolm did not oppose their presence—he only asked them to serve him. Walcher, bishop of Durham, was fully aware that he had to maintain good relations between the Scots and the English. This was not easy where different tongues were involved—Gaelic, French and English—

and the bishop may have hoped the monks' presence would have helped. But, after much correspondence, Bishop Walcher, concerned for their safety, threatened "to excommunicate [Aldwin and Turgot] ... in the presence of the most holy body of St Cuthbert, unless they should return to him and remain under St Cuthbert's protection".[30] So they returned.

The reaction of the Scottish queen, Margaret, may have been quite different. She desired to convert the church she had built at Dunfermline Palace into a monastery and would have welcomed the advice of the monks. This may have been the first occasion that she heard of Aldwin and Turgot (see chapter 7).

When they returned from Melrose in 1078, Bishop Walcher bestowed on Aldwin and Turgot the *vill* and ruins of Monkwearmouth, destroyed by Malcolm in 1071.[31] Aldwin thus became abbot of both Jarrow and Monkwearmouth. They made themselves "dwellings out of twigs ... [and] worked to clear out the church of St Peter, of which only the walls were still standing in a semi-ruinous state, and they cut down the trees and cleared the creepers and thorn-bushes which had completely taken it over. Then they roofed it ... ".[32]

A steady flow of postulants to the revived foundations continued, and Turgot felt a similar call to spiritual and intellectual adventure. His vocation had been tested and Aldwin gave him the monastic habit of a Benedictine monk "and with affection as his dearest brother in Christ, taught him by word and example how sweet it is to carry the yoke of Christ".[33] They were joined by men from the remotest parts of England to live the monastic life with them. Bishop Walcher "loved them with all his heart like a benign father, and he often deigned to visit them himself, and generously to give them whatever they lacked".[34] The bishop was not a monk, but he embraced them and "often called them to confer with him; and sometimes he received their advice and most willingly condescended to obey their instructions".[35] Aldwin and Turgot were frequently called to Durham to consult with the bishop. These journeys would have been momentous occasions. As they approached the cathedral, the towers must have dominated the site—a satisfying sight for two weary travel-stained riders.

Bishop Walcher

Archbishop Lanfranc (1070–89) was leading reforming movements in the Church in England, with new canon law enforcing celibacy on priests and encouraging a more austere form of monastic life. At this time Durham Cathedral was served by clerks who did not follow a Rule of Life, and many were married priests. Walcher himself was not a monk but a cleric "of Lotharingian race, exceedingly well instructed in divine and secular knowledge".[36] He imposed upon the *congregatio* the customs of secular canons with the intention of forming a community to observe the daytime and night-time offices. He was pleased that he now had Benedictine monks within his diocese.

Walcher began laying out a central cloister to be surrounded with monastic buildings.[37] This had become a central feature of European monastic architecture, but was not found in Celtic houses.

In 1074, following the deposition from power of Earl Waltheof, Bishop Walcher was also created earl of Northumbria.[38] This gave him additional responsibilities for law and order and for leading the local militia, though responsibility for the latter was deputed to a kinsman of the bishop, named Gilbert, who was appointed sheriff. The bishop benefited from the advice of a local magnate called Ligulf (Liulph), who had fled north when the Normans arrived, and had married Ealdgyth, the daughter of a previous earl of Northumbria, Ealdred of Bamburgh (killed 1038). Walcher had a high regard for Ligulf and relied on him to represent the Northumbrians on the bishop's councils. Walcher also depended heavily on his chaplain Leobwin, and there were frequent clashes between Ligulf and the chaplain. Finally Leobwin incited Gilbert to kill Ligulf. Gilbert took soldiers from his own and the bishop's retinues and slaughtered Ligulf and his family in their own home. Walcher was furious and rebuked his chaplain, telling him that, as a result of his deeds and foolish plots, "you have destroyed both me, and yourself, and all my family".[39]

A general council was called for Thursday 14 May 1080 at Gateshead to settle differences. The bishop offered to hold a legal enquiry on behalf of the victims' families, but the people were not satisfied and attacked the bishop. The bishop, Gilbert, Leobwin and many of the bishop's household were killed. The chief instigator of the foment was Eadulf Rus, son of Uhtred, but Walcher's downfall was due to his inability to control his soldiers. Walcher's naked body was found by monks from Jarrow, who conveyed it by water to their monastery nearby, and thence to Durham, where it was buried in the chapter house.[40]

"When news of what had been done spread far and wide, Bishop Odo of Bayeux [the king's half-brother], who was then second only to the king, came to Durham with many of the leading men of the kingdom and a large force of armed men; and in avenging the death of the bishop virtually laid the land waste".[41]

Bishop William of St-Calais

The king, realising that the roles of bishop and military leader could not be effectively combined, appointed first Aubrey (Alberic) de Courcy, and then Robert de Mowbray, as earl of Northumbria, in order to subdue the Northumbrians. In November 1080 King William asked his son Robert to build a new castle on the Tyne at Monkchester, opposite the site of Walcher's murder. The king appointed William of St-Calais (Carilef) to be bishop of Durham on 9 November 1080, and he was consecrated on Sunday 3 January 1081 at Gloucester by the archbishop of York.[42]

The new bishop was devoted to the cult of St Calais, a sixth-century hermit (feast-day 1 July), perhaps because his father, a knight, spent his last days at the abbey of St-Calais in Maine. William himself was prior there until appointed abbot of St-Vincent, just outside Le Mans, in 1078.[43] There he impressed the king as being a strong and powerful ecclesiastic. He was the first Norman to be appointed bishop of Durham, and, like Aldwin and Turgot, he was a Benedictine, following the same Rule, and ready to serve Durham and to follow the traditions of the cult of St Cuthbert. The bishop supported the work of the monks in restoring the former monasteries in Northumbria and gave them the *vill* of Southwick, near Wearmouth.[44]

Bishop William was a strong leader and by his wisdom and energy he defended the rights, laws and privileges of the Church so that during his lifetime "they could not be infringed or violated" by anyone.[45] He was a good debater with a capacious memory and possessed administrative capability which the king used to help him govern England. He had the king's complete confidence, and his name appears as a senior witness to many royal charters.[46] William of Malmesbury (c.1125) described him as "a ruthless orator of dangerous ambitions".[47]

When he arrived in the north "he found the saint's land virtually desolate, and he perceived that the place which the saint renders illustrious by the presence of his body was shamefully destitute and provided with a degree of service inappropriate to his sanctity. For he found neither monks of his own order, nor regular canons".[48] The state of the countryside was no doubt due to the ravaging by Odo of Bayeux following the murder in 1080 of Bishop Walcher.[49]

Bishop William realised the importance of St Cuthbert, and was conscious of the lack of professed monks to regulate and maintain his shrine. He wished to found a monastery at Durham in order to safeguard Cuthbert's shrine, so he conferred with Thomas, archbishop of York (1070–1100), concerning this. The archbishop issued an edict to gain support for the project, reporting that he had spent a night beside the tomb of St Cuthbert, where he had received a vision and had been healed of his infirmities.[50]

In September 1082 the bishop was in Normandy and perhaps it was then that he explained to the king the changes he envisaged at Durham.[51] The king was delighted by the bishop's plan to eliminate the secular clerks at Durham. No doubt he remembered his embarrassing experience at Durham in 1072 (see p. 12). King William suggested that the pope be acquainted with the situation and his approval sought for changes to the *congregatio* of St Cuthbert that had preserved the cult for almost 400 years. The *congregatio* consisted of priests, many of them married, and

▶ *A supplicant is healed by a touch from St Cuthbert, from Raine* Cuthbert *p. 71. Based on an illuminated manuscript of Bede's* Life of St Cuthbert *c.1200 (now London, British Library, Yates Thompson MS 26).*

perhaps still living in the residences in the town assigned by lot to their ancestors by Bishop Aldhun.[52] Although they preserved the cult of St Cuthbert and fulfilled the liturgical uses handed down through the years at Lindisfarne, they had degenerated into a body following family traditions which involved hereditary prebends. Pope Gregory VII probably suggested the amalgamation of Jarrow and Monkwearmouth, centred on Durham, to concentrate resources. The pope approved the proposals and issued letters of excommunication to be served on any who obstructed them. The pope also sent letters to King William and Archbishop Lanfranc, asking them to assist the bishop in setting up Durham monastery. Bishop William made exhaustive enquiries on the age-old relationship between the bishop and clerks before completing arrangements.[53]

The ancient community was naturally resistant to changes and most of the clerks did not wish to become monks, only one offering to adopt the Benedictine habit.[54] The congregatio had become powerful, but it was important to retain the cult of St Cuthbert, so Bishop William provided churches in stone for the dispossessed clerks, at Auckland (St Andrew), Darlington (St Cuthbert), Easington and Norton (both St Mary).[55] The former treasurer, Eilaf, decided to return to Hexham, which had become a ruin, and was provost there from 1085 to 1090.[56]

On Friday 26 May 1083 the monks at Jarrow and Monkwearmouth moved to Durham to create a new monastery of twenty-three monks.[57] The bishop called a meeting of the cathedral chapter on 31 May and became the titular abbot. Aldwin was made the first prior, and Leofwin, "a prudent man who greatly feared God", was made sacristan.[58]

The bishop of Durham had semi-regal powers, for it was he and not the king who collected taxes, fines, farm profits, etc. The Saxon palatine authority was in force, and the cathedral and castle now represented the spiritual and temporal power of the land. The bishop had to assess a fair distribution of the revenues of the enormous estates of St Cuthbert among the clerks, the monastic community and himself. "He segregated his own landed possessions from theirs, so that the monks should possess their lands for the purpose of their maintenance and clothing, entirely free and quit of episcopal service and of all customary exactions".[59]

The king spent Christmas 1085 at Gloucester and held court for five days, and then for three days discussed church matters with the bishops. He had "great discussion and very deep speech with his counsellors about this land—how it was occupied, and by what men. He then sent his men over all England into each shire, and had it made out how many hides of land were in the shire . . . ".[60] The bishop of Durham, William of St-Calais, was present and was given the task of organising the survey and compiling the results.[61]

Work on the compilation took Bishop William away from Durham until its completion in September 1087.[62] In his absence more responsibility devolved on the prior, a role that was soon to pass to Turgot.

The Domesday survey

The bishop was blessed with intelligence and persuasive ability. He divided the country into manageable circuits, with commissioners seeking answers to their detailed enquiries by empanelling jurors under oath. Commissioners were sent to areas where they held no land, and Bishop William covered circuits I and II, the counties of Berkshire, Cornwall, Devon, Dorset, Hampshire, Kent, Somerset, Surrey, Sussex and Wiltshire.

It was a huge undertaking and required exceptional administrative skills of "the man behind the survey".[63] Speed in compiling information was essential; any delay would involve inevitable changes, making entries invalid. Lands were frequently changing hands and the death of an important tenant could involve many properties. Regardless of the language used at the hundred courts, final verdicts were written in Latin, often by men who spoke Norman French and knew little English. Everyone was classified as a freeman, sokeman, villein, bordar, cottar or slave.

There is strong evidence that the main scribe of the Great Domesday, who wrote the list of contents, held a position of some importance in the Durham scriptorium.[64] There are a number of distinctive features in his handwriting that also appear in works connected to Durham.

On 1 August 1086 the king forced all his followers who had been granted lands in England to swear allegiance to him at Old Sarum.[65] At the same time the king received a progress report on the survey.

The result of the findings for the south-western circuit became the *Liber Exoniensis* (Exeter book), which may have been only a draft survey as there are many erasures and corrections. The entry for Taunton, Somerset, includes holdings of the bishop of Winchester, with a note that the king had made a grant of lands "as he himself recognised at Salisbury in the hearing of the Bishop of Durham, whom he commanded to write this his grant in the returns". The same statement is repeated in the Great Domesday Book,[66] which incorporates all the south-western results but in a condensed text.

Northumberland and Durham were not included in the survey, probably as they were not firmly under Norman control and there were no shire courts from which to gather information. Most English counties had changed from earldoms to sheriffdoms but Robert de Mowbray was still earl of Northumbria, and although he had his own sheriff, Morel, the bishop of Durham had no difficulty in resisting the workings of the shires.

The Domesday survey for Lincolnshire reveals that, before the Conquest, a Thorgot (sometimes Thorgot Lag) had held land spread across Lindsey with over 8 hides in the west riding (Bransby, Buslingthorpe, Corringham and Fillingham), 45 acres in the north riding (Holton le Clay and Thorganby), and 5½ hides in the south riding (Benniworth and Wickenby).[67] If these refer to our Turgot, he had been a minor feudal lord and would have been able to hold positions of influence.

CHAPTER 3

Turgot the Prior

Prior Aldwin died on 12 April 1087 and was mourned by the monks as one who was "a good and modest man, one of whom the church had great need for his prudence and counsel, and very conscientious in all things lest he offend God".[1] "By common counsel of the brothers the bishop rightly appointed Turgot his disciple in his place as prior, and ordered him to direct the care of the entire monastery within and without in a God-fearing way".[2]

The life of the prior of a cathedral monastery was not easy and his duties were onerous. Turgot was now responsible for the worship, the finances, and the repair of buildings, as well as the discipline, education and spiritual support of the monks, not only those within the monastery but those in outlying cells around Northumbria. There would have been about seventy monks under his control, some based at cells such as Jarrow, Monkwearmouth, Lindisfarne, Farne, Finchale and Crayke. Some forty generally resided in the cathedral monastery, and thirty in the dependencies.

Under Turgot were officers with specialised duties. The sacristan had custody of all relics, ornaments, vestments and service books. The precentor was responsible for services in the choir, the succentor for singing and the music and the direction of the choir school. The cellarer provided all supplies of food and drink, and the kitchener prepared the food, with the refectorer ensuring order in the dining hall. The chamberlain provided bedding, clothing and boots. The infirmarer attended the sick and aged, while the *circator* patrolled the cloister to ensure silence, tidiness and security. Their combined efforts made certain that the daily mass was performed, and the monastic offices sung in the choir.

Turgot has been credited with introducing from Norway the custom of carrying in procession the shrine "wherin ye bones of ye holie man St Beede was inshryned",[3] with other relics, on Ascension Day, Whit Sunday and Trinity Sunday. According to the late sixteenth-century text, *Rites of Durham*, the route had begun at the north door of the cathedral, crossed the churchyard, went down the North Bailey, passing St Mary's Church, as far as the abbey gatehouse, "where a grete number of people did stand both men, women, & childrine, wth great reverence and devoc'on, wch was a goodly & a godly sight to behold", and returned via the abbey garth and the cloisters to the south door of the church.[4] Turgot would have been familiar with a similar custom at Niðaróss, "where, from the beginning, it was the custom to bear the shrine of St Olaf round the town, probably because the older churches . . . were too small and unable to hold the many pilgrims on St Olaf's Day, so as to allow them to approach the shrine, standing as it did in the small single-aisled chancel at the top of the church. This custom at Durham, exceptional in England until after 1154, was undoubtedly taken from Niðaróss by prior Turgot".[5]

Turgot was now a priest and, as the superior of the monastery, could administer the sacraments, wear pontificals and hear confessions. In addition, while the bishop was superintending the compilation of the Domesday survey, which entailed prolonged absences from Durham, Prior Turgot acted as senior cleric in the diocese.

The bishop sent letters to the monastery during his absence from Durham, encouraging the community to pray for him and not to abandon their vocations. In one letter he urged strict adherence to the Rule, good behaviour, frequent confession and full meetings of the daily chapter. He explained that "he was prevented by the king's affairs",[6] and asked that this letter be read weekly in chapter during his absence. The letters imply that Turgot had been left with a great degree of freedom of action.

The Durham antiquarian, William Hutchinson, observes that "the monastery profited greatly by [Turgot's] prudent government; the privileges were enlarged, and revenues considerably increased by his influence; and he promoted many improvements in the sacred edifices".[7]

Turgot inherited a remarkable scriptorium (writing area), and a few of its scribes had assisted in writing up Domesday Book. There had been little time for a tradition to have been built up and few of the monks had experience in transcription or illustration. The sixteenth-century author of the *Rites of Durham* recalled that the walk adjoining the church was set aside as the scriptorium with, "in every wyndowe iij° pewes or carrells where every one of the old monks had his Carrell severall by him selfe".[8] While the scriptorium was good, the muniment room was poor, as can be seen from the following example.

Robert de Mowbray, earl of Northumbria, had relinquished all rights over the land of St Cuthbert,[9] but in 1090 he gave Tynemouth monastery to the monks of St Albans.[10] This was one of the early Celtic monasteries, destroyed by the Danes in 875 but refounded by Earl Waltheof II in 1075, and repaired by monks from Jarrow. It was regarded as part of the Cuthbert community under Jarrow, and in 1083 became a cell of Durham. The loss of Tynemouth may have been due to the lack of charters in the Durham muniments. During the reign of William I, Bishop William of St-Calais was often absent from Durham on the king's business. This may have resulted in a failure to set up the Durham monastery with a royal charter, with benefactors, and attested charters confirming ownership of property, and may have given rise to a series of charter forgeries at Durham in the second half of the twelfth century. A diploma of Bishop William, purporting to deal with the foundation and endowment of the monastery, has been found to be a forgery.[11]

Bishop in exile

When King William died near Rouen, France, on 9 September 1087, his second eldest surviving son, William Rufus, was already on his way to England to claim the crown. He was anointed by Lanfranc on 26 September and William of St-Calais "was added to the company of the king's friends and made a prelate of England. But he did not remain in the favour of the king".[12]

Many barons rebelled against the new king, considering that the eldest son of the Conqueror, Robert Curthose, would serve them better than William Rufus. The bishop of Durham jeopardised his position by not attending the royal court, which the king regarded as an act of treason, breaking his oath of fealty. The bishop was accused of not supporting the king in resisting the conspiring Odo of Bayeux, thus giving comfort to the king's enemies.[13]

The king ordered the confiscation of the bishop's lands on 12 March 1088. The bishop had meetings with the king in June and July but without favourable result.

He managed to reach the safety of Durham Castle to consider his position. The trial of the bishop took place at Old Sarum on 2 November, when his defence relied on canon law. He refused to be subject to lay judgement but sought justice from bishops in canon law. He produced a copy of extracts from canons known to historians as the *Collectio Lanfranci*,[14] which state that a person despoiled of his possessions must have them restored to him before judicial proceedings could begin. The king's answer was, "You may talk as you please, still you shall not escape out of my hands, until you have delivered up the castle to me".[15] The importance to the king of the power of Durham is clear.

There is no evidence that his fellow bishops supported the arguments of the bishop of Durham. Lanfranc maintained that he had seen no royal writ disseizing him of his bishopric, and that canon law was not relevant, as they were making judgement concerning his fief and not his bishopric.

The result was that the bishop's estates were confiscated on 14 November and the army sent by William Rufus took Durham Castle on 13 December.[16] It had a retinue of at least 100 knights.[17] The castle was in the king's hands from 1089 to 1091.

It must have been a fearful time for Prior Turgot and the monks, especially when they learned that the bishop had left England and was exiled to Normandy. The monks "feared that they would suffer many adversities" from the king without the safeguard of their bishop but, "contrary to these fears they were protected by God, who had mercy on them because of the merits of St Cuthbert, so that no adversity harmed them, and they found the king himself reasonably kindly towards them. For although in other monasteries and churches he behaved more harshly, he not only took nothing from them, but even gave them of his own, and as his father had done he defended them from the injuries of the malevolent".[18]

The bishop was warmly received in Normandy by the king's elder brother, Duke Robert, who appointed him to the chief post in the administration of the duchy, a position he held until 1091.[19] He spent his time, not only in administering, but in trying to improve relations among the three royal brothers, William Rufus, Robert of Normandy and the future Henry I.

He also amassed books and manuscripts for Durham monastery and began making plans for a new cathedral there in expectation of his return.

Turgot in charge

When he had become prior of Durham, Turgot must have stopped to evaluate the state of the Northumbrian Church, and in particular the importance of Durham Cathedral. Everyone knew that the Church in Northumbria was strong, with an abundance of ancient charters, and many preserved bodies of saints. Legends of the saints abounded throughout the land. Yet there had been panic-stricken flights by monastic communities, with their relics, from the Viking invaders. These journeys lasted longer than the cause. Could this arise from fear of failure or of death? Did superstition govern their motives? Why were the relics so important? Did the relics provide power and prestige?

The *congregatio* of St Cuthbert had been proud of their achievements, had always followed the example of the saint, and were mindful of his presence at all times. As they journeyed they had with them, not only the body of Cuthbert, but Æthelred's stone cross of 730, the Lindisfarne Gospels, the gifts given in 934 by King Athelstan, many other relics, the gospel book of John and the *Liber Vitae* containing names of members and benefactors. Ownership of the estates of St Cuthbert provided their support.

Now the *congregatio* was no more, and Turgot had to bear the responsibility of all this. He had to unite the brethren to support him and to enthuse them with new opportunities. They knew that they had had a great past, and were surrounded by evidence of ancient greatness. Turgot reminded them that they had survived what could have been a turbulent change with the Norman Conquest. Their way of life remained relatively intact. He was able to show that it had been no more than a tremor in the long development of monasticism.

The king fully appreciated the importance of the cathedral, situated as it was in a region where the king of Scotland had great influence and which was virtually outside Norman control, but which looked to Durham for spiritual leadership. There was never any clash between the kings of England and the cathedral, but frequently between the king and the Northumbrian nobility who resisted the attempts of the Normans to govern the north. The local lords living north of the river Tees were alarmed at the 'harrying' of the land and naturally encouraged the revolts of 1069 (which began in Durham), and those of 1074–75 and 1080. The area was remote from the centre of power, so that Norman influence was always weak.

Now Turgot represented the Church in the north, performing pastoral and liturgical functions as a bishop. He even attended the *curia regis* on behalf of the bishop, and the king, understanding the responsibilities being undertaken on his behalf, accorded him special courtesies—William Rufus rose humbly "and commanded him in all things to attend to the care of the church in complete liberty under himself as he would have done under the bishop".[20] The king was reported to have been uncharacteristically generous to the church at Durham.

It was on a journey to the royal court that Turgot was involved in one of Cuthbert's miracles. The prior, accompanied by two of the monks, sought shelter for the night at a village. The monks and their saint were mocked by a householder, who collapsed "as if dead", but was finally restored to life by St Cuthbert. News of the event caused great amusement when recounted at the royal court.[21]

The prior thus gained a position of considerable influence and freedom during the bishop's absence.

During the bishop's banishment Turgot began to build the monastic offices that were the responsibility of the monks.[22] They included the undercroft and main floor of the dining hall, which he sited on the south side of the cloister. This early development fixed the southern limit of the cloister. Here, outside the dining hall, was the washing place (*lavatorium*). No doubt Turgot was responsible for building the conduit to provide the water. He may have continued work on the important chapter house and adjoining monks' prison, thought to have been begun by Bishop Walcher. A small triangular window still remains.

The monk Reginald of Durham (*fl.*1162–1173) tells of an attempted theft from this dining hall. Rodbert, son of the master cook, obtained access into the refectory, through the kitchen or buttery window, during the night, and filled a bag with plate and linen. Hanging above the prior's table was a bell, called a *schyll*, used to summon the brethren to meals. It was "of antient workmanship, having in it more of brass than of tin", and rung by means of a cord. It was believed to have belonged to St Cuthbert, so Prior Turgot had had it "splendidly ornamented with gold", but the thief thought it was of pure gold, and attempted to remove it, with a predictable result.[23]

The king visits the north

Malcolm of Scotland invaded Northumbria in May 1091 and reached as far south as Chester-le-Street, "but an inconsiderable military force assembled against him, and caused him speedily to retire from fear".[24] It was felt that Durham had been saved by the power of prayer and St Cuthbert's intervention. In August the royal brothers, William and Robert, now briefly reconciled, crossed from Normandy to attack Scotland. William Rufus stopped at Durham, where he restored William of St-Calais to the bishopric, in return for his good offices as mediator in Normandy.[25] Edgar the Ætheling, brother-in-law to the Scottish king, mediated between Scotland and the Norman royal brothers for three days while William Rufus was at Durham. Malcolm, king of Scotland, refused to pay homage to the English king, but agreed to serve Robert, duke of Normandy, arguing that he could not serve two masters.[26]

The duke was happy with Malcolm's decision and returned to Normandy on 23 December 1091. William Rufus, mindful of his rejection, set out in the spring of 1092 and annexed Cumbria, including Carlisle, where he built a castle to guard the Eden crossing, and re-populated the area, which was placed in the diocese of Durham. Malcolm objected to this as Cumbria was under the protection of Strathclyde. He sought a meeting with the English king. William Rufus replied by asking Edgar the Ætheling to go to Scotland and escort Malcolm to attend the royal court at Gloucester in the following August.[27]

Exiled bishop returns

Symeon says the bishop was reinstated on 11 September 1091, whereas the tract *De iniusta vexacione Willelmi episcopi* seems to suggest 14 November 1091. The confusion might have arisen from the fact that 11 September 1092 was the day site-clearing began for the new cathedral, according to the next sentence of the tract.[28]

While William of St-Calais was in exile he was moved to rebuild Durham Cathedral on his return. He probably visited Bernay near Lisieux, built in the mid-eleventh century, and noted the three apsed chapels in echelon. He may have spoken to the mason who was decorating the underside of the presbytery arches with 'soffit rolls', the first known examples. Perhaps he visited Jumièges and noticed the major piers of the nave, alternating with cylindrical minor piers, and also the tall arcade above, with a low tribune or gallery.

The bishop had sent on ahead of him gold and silver altar vessels and vestments, together with an impressive collection of forty-six books.[29] The volumes are listed on the flyleaf of a Bible he had made in Normandy for use at Durham. Other books purchased in Normandy had been specially illustrated for him. One capital initial shows William of St-Calais as patron and Robert Benjamin as artist. There were works of theology, service books and texts suitable for use at chapter assemblies.[30] Hutchinson suggested that, "not content with giving these rich presents and noble ornaments, he brought over from Normandy the plan of a new church, devised in the style and magnificence used on the continent", but modern scholars do not think a physical plan existed.[31]

An agreement was quickly reached with the monastery. The bishop as patron would be responsible for paying for the construction of the cathedral from his own diocesan resources. The monks would provide for their own conventual requirements.[32]

A twelfth-century source claimed that the bishop re-granted to the monastery the borough of Elvet, Durham, "where the monks should have forty merchants houses or tradesmen's shops, distinct and separate from the bishop's borough of Durham, that they might trade there, freed from duties payable to the bishop and his successors".[33]

The bishop's involvement with the Domesday survey continued, and after his return from exile he witnessed every writ of the royal court containing a reference to the survey.

Unfortunately the bishop again became involved in trying to reconcile further differences between the two royal brothers—Robert and William Rufus. He returned to Normandy in January 1092, to confer with Robert while the king was in Cumbria. William of St-Calais was still in Normandy in February 1092, but was witnessing charters of William Rufus later in 1092.[34] He was still absent from Durham on 3 February 1093, when he attended the funeral of Geoffrey of Coutances, but he had returned to Durham by August to attend the laying of foundation stones for the new cathedral.

He "did pull it all downe"

William of St-Calais, being of continental origin himself and deeming the Anglo-Saxon structure to be, in the words of Durham antiquarian, William Hutchinson, "not of suitable magnificence to the dignity and increasing power of the See, formed a plan for a new erection, similar to the superb structures he had seen on the continent".[35] The bishop was fortunate in having a prior with useful experience, for Turgot, as we have seen, had spent time with cathedral builders in Norway.[36] No doubt a meeting was held with the bishop as patron, the mason as builder, and the prior who would supervise the project, to agree the optimum size of the building: the total length east to west; the length of the transepts north to south; the siting of the high altar; the choir; and the shrine of St Cuthbert. They would have assessed the resources required—of men, money and materials.

The whole community was informed of the proposals and enjoined to work for the good of the cathedral, to maintain monastic traditions, the cult of St Cuthbert, and the prosperity of the Cuthbert estates. The mason could now start working on a detailed plan, and the requirements for the foundations.

The bishop, "beinge not well content with the smalnesse and homelinesse of that buildinge did pull it all downe".[37] Though written 500 years after the event described, these words probably echo the regret of some of the monks at the destruction of Aldhun's cathedral, built 995–1018, which began on 11 September 1092.[38] A complete demolition was unusual in England, although normal on the continent—hence, no doubt, the special mention by the chroniclers. Modern historians now suggest that only a partial demolition took place at first.[39] The west tower and adjacent porticus, built 1020–1042, may have been temporarily reprieved to assist in maintaining canonical services, time being marked by the ringing of bells at the canonical hours, which varied according to the length of daylight. The sanctuary might also have survived until 1104 to house Cuthbert's remains. The "faire and beautifull tombe of stone in the cloyster garth a yeard high [3 feet or 0.9m] from the ground, where St Cuthb: was laid untill his shrine was prepared for him in the new church that now is" survived into the sixteenth century,[40] and was then sometimes described as occupying the same position that it had in "the White Church".[41] The accounts of the opening of Cuthbert's coffin before it was transferred into the new building seem to describe a substantial chapel with the shrine located behind the altar (see pp. 44–47).

Durham was not the only cathedral entirely demolished to make way for a Norman replacement.[42] Demolition of the Saxon Old Minster at Winchester began in July 1093, although part of the new structure had been built in 1079 and occupied in April 1093. With the arrival of the new Romanesque tastes and techniques, old buildings were swept away. It was Goscelin of St-Bertin, who came to England in 1058, who declared that "he destroys well, who builds something better . . .".[43]

We may wonder why, if it was to be a larger structure, it could not have been built around the existing cathedral. It seems likely that the new work was immediately to the north of the Saxon structure.[44] No doubt Turgot remembered the problems over the foundations at Niðaróss, Norway, where existing foundations were insufficient for the pillars supporting a stone-vaulted roof.

Excavation for new foundations began on Friday 29 July 1093,[45] after the brothers had said prayers. Solid rock was reached easily and digging was completed in less than a fortnight. The pillars and walls of Durham Cathedral rest on foundations made over nine centuries ago. Because of the steepness and soil structure at the east end of the site, the builder found it necessary to build deeper foundations to support the eastern apses.[46]

The archdeaconry

Also in 1093 the bishop led Prior Turgot before "the people of the whole bishopric and enjoined him to be his representative over them, so that through the office of archdeacon he should exercise pastoral care in all things throughout the bishopric, and he decreed that whoever might succeed him as prior should similarly assume the office of archdeacon".[47] This confirmed a status already existing, for Turgot had been acting as archdeacon from 1088 when the bishop was sent for trial by King William Rufus. According to William of Malmesbury (c.1125), the prior was "second in command for the whole bishopric".[48] Symeon of Durham remarks that he was to discharge the function of a preacher.[49] As archdeacon, Turgot was now given special powers and privileges, and could preside over synods in the absence of the bishop. He was now officially the deputy of the bishop in the diocese as well as his deputy, as abbot, in the monastery. No doubt the bishop wished to avoid any clash of interests between two deputies by amalgamating the posts.

To administer the whole of the diocese was unusual, as normally an archdeacon undertook to serve only part of a diocese. At this time, the diocese included East Lothian, Hexhamshire and Cumbria. When William Rufus annexed Cumbria in 1092 it was intended that it should be in St Cuthbert's see which had connections with the area back in the seventh century.[50] A royal writ of 1094 ordered "W. son of Thierry and all the King's lieges of Carlisle and all who abode beyond the Lowther to accept spiritual jurisdiction of the bishop and archdeacon of Durham". A further writ, after the bishop's death, refers solely to the archdeacon.[51]

At Jedburgh, in Lothian, Eadulf Rus, the murderer of Bishop Walcher in 1080, had been buried after being killed by a woman.[52] His body was disinterred and "cast out by command of Turgot, when prior of Durham, and left to rot upon the earth".[53]

Prior Turgot realised the importance of seeking the patronage of the Scottish king for peace and unity with England, and knew that Malcolm and his queen, Margaret, would wish to confirm blessings to and from the community of St Cuthbert. Margaret was terminally ill and keen to solemnise a *conventio* (bond of confraternity) between the Scottish royal house and the Durham community.[54] King Malcolm agreed to a public demonstration of a new bond with St Cuthbert.

Edgar the Ætheling, Queen Margaret's brother, arrived at Durham in August 1093, having been sent to accompany Malcolm to Gloucester for the royal court. On 11 August, Malcolm was invited to lay a foundation stone of the new cathedral. He was the only layman to take part in the ceremony.[55] In fact these stones were laid by a Norman bishop, an English prior and a Scottish king.

The bishop of Durham, Edgar the Ætheling and King Malcolm arrived at the court at Gloucester on 24 August, but the meeting between the two kings never took place. Malcolm was informed that his plea had to go before the *curia regis* and the judgement of the barons. Malcolm maintained that he could not make amends on the border issue without the judgement of the barons of both kingdoms.[56]

There were other important items to be discussed at the royal court, including the appointment of a new archbishop of Canterbury. William Rufus had procrastinated following the death of Lanfranc in 1079 but, struck with a sudden and violent illness and fearing death, he offered the primacy to Anselm, abbot of Bec, who was initially reluctant to accept, probably on the 'advice' of the bishop of Durham. The bishop attended Anselm's investiture at Canterbury in September 1093.[57]

Bishop William was present at the 1093 Christmas court of William Rufus at Gloucester and secured a charter allowing him to hold in free alms all the lands in England for which he had previously owed military service.[58]

On 11 February 1094 Bishop William was present with William Rufus at the consecration of Battle Abbey.[59] At that time the king was waiting to send an army to Normandy against Duke Robert.

In 1094 Anselm wished to go to Rome to receive the pallium from Urban II, but William Rufus did not recognise Urban as pope and refused his permission. The matter was to be resolved at the Council of Rockingham, which met 25 to 27 February 1095, when the bishop of Durham spoke for the king, but Anselm persisted in his obedience to Urban.[60] The Council came to an inconclusive end, and relations between the king and the bishop of Durham became strained. This marked the end of the bishop's public career. He performed his last episcopal duty in Northumbria with Prior Turgot on 29 August 1095 in the cemetery of Norham church on the Scottish border, when they confirmed the gift to St Cuthbert by Edgar, son of Malcolm and Margaret, of lands in Lothian.[61]

The death of Bishop William

In the summer of 1095 King William Rufus captured Robert de Mowbray, earl of Northumbria, at Tynemouth. He was in a conspiracy to transfer the English crown to Count Stephen of Aumâle (Albemarle), a distant member of the royal family.[62] The bishop of Durham and the earl must have met with each other on occasion, and the king may have suspected an alliance. Bishop William was asked to appear at the Christmas court of William Rufus on an unspecified charge, but he fell ill on arrival. He was comforted by the primates of Canterbury and York and the bishops of Winchester and of Bath and Wells.[63]

Even on his deathbed men came to visit and seek his advice. He was given the last sacraments on 1 January 1096 and died the next day. His body was conveyed from Windsor to Durham on a litter borne by horses. His belongings included five copes, three chasubles with a large stole and maniple, embroidered at the end, an altar cloth, a small silver censer, a small silver pitcher, two bronze-gilt candlesticks and a small silver candlestick.[64] The journey took almost a fortnight. The bishop had made clear that he would not allow his corruptible remains to be laid in the same building as the incorrupt body of St Cuthbert, and he was buried in the chapter house, beside Bishop Walcher, on 16 January,[65] wearing a gold-embroidered robe ornamented with griffins.[66] The brethren grieved at his death, and Symeon of Durham wrote of the monks' sorrow, "I believe . . . that there was not one among them who would not have redeemed the bishop's life with his own if he could have done so".[67]

But in spite of this profession of grief, there is a sense of disappointment in Symeon's assessment of the bishop. "Much of what Symeon has to say about William of St-Calais's achievements has this hollow ring to it. It is almost as though Symeon felt obliged to praise St-Calais but there was something preventing his whole-hearted endorsement of his regime. That something was Bishop William's comparative neglect of his bishopric and the monastery at Durham".[68]

Perhaps the vision of Boso sums up the view of the monks.[69] Symeon recounts how a knight in the bishop's household in the castle, named Boso, became ill and lay in a trance for three days. He experienced a vision and, when recovered enough, secretly approached Prior Turgot in order to unburden his thoughts. The knight had been led by a mysterious guide through both pleasant and dreadful places and then saw a procession of the monks in strict ceremonial order, except that two were out of line. All were chanting, and the crucifer bore a glittering cross, but ahead was a huge wall lacking any doors or windows. The procession passed through it and Boso found a very small window from which he saw a field full of people. In the foreground were proud Northumbrian spearmen on well-fed horses but they vanished like smoke. These were replaced by prancing Norman knights on chargers filling the field with a clank of armour. These disappeared as though the earth had opened and swallowed them up. The scene then filled with a multitude of women, and Boso realised that these were priest's wives, awaiting the fires of hell. His next vision was an area containing a single tall iron building, the door of which kept opening and closing. Bishop William of St-Calais suddenly appeared and asked for his attorney, brother Gosfrid. "He should be with me here at the trial," he said.

No dream has a logical explanation of all its facets, but some parts may be found to bear some truth. The two backsliding monks were apparently discovered out of line and Turgot was able to warn them in time. Spectacular well-trained knights appear, as well as men transported to battle sites on overfed cart-horses. The bishop was controlling his diocese from a fortress and was busy with many comings and goings. The castle was increasing in strength and height, while beside it a vast cathedral was quickly rising, enabling processions to enter the unfinished, unvaulted shell. Disciplined monks were better than secular canons with wives. All this was taken as a portent of the imminent death of the bishop.

Symeon adds that the bishop "trembled in great fear, and began thenceforth to take greater care of the health of his soul, being more generous in alms-giving, praying at greater length and more intently, and not setting aside on account of any business the periods reserved for daily prayer in private".[70]

Symeon ends his record with the death of the bishop on 2 January 1096, swiftly followed by the death of brother Gosfrid. The vision probably took place in 1094 and the bishop was unwell throughout 1095.

The contribution of William of St-Calais to the see of Durham was great. He set up the monastery and began to reorganise the revenues for the cathedral, both episcopal and monastic. He satisfied the needs of the monastery, not only financially but with service books, ornaments and other necessities. Although an ambitious man, he lived a simple life, possessing talent and great learning. "His sternness was not rigid nor his gentleness lax . . . making his severity jocund and his jocundity severe".[71]

However, the death of the bishop brought to an end the agreement of 1092 (see p. 30). In the decade before his death he had been too busy to make firm arrangements for the provisioning of the monastery, and he died before implementation of his plans to provide further endowments.[72] The bishop's constant attendance at the royal court had already become a strain on the planning and financial requirements for the new cathedral.

Often churches controlled by monastic communities claimed to be exempt from episcopal control. At Durham the interests of the bishop and the monks were in complete harmony, due to the considerable influence and freedom of the prior within the bishopric. Turgot was able to safeguard the "lands, men, [and] customs" of the bishopric during the interregnum.[73] A royal writ instructed the king's sheriff and vassals of Carlisle to obey Turgot, the archdeacon of Durham "in matters spiritual . . . as they did in the time of W[illiam] bishop of Durham".[74]

Ranulf Flambard buys the bishopric

The bishopric remained vacant until 1099, the king being loath to make an appointment that would bring to an end his income from the vacant see, which amounted to £300 a year.[75] In 1099 he accepted the offer of £1000 from his agent, Ranulf Flambard,[76] who was consecrated as bishop of Durham on 5 June.[77] However, within fifteen months the king was dead, and Flambard was arrested and imprisoned, though he soon escaped and fled to Normandy.[78]

Following Flambard's arrest, Turgot was left in charge of the diocese once again, which involved preaching, visitations, patronage and consecration of new churches, and investing priests. With an absent bishop he had been administering the spiritualities of the see virtually from 1088 and would do so almost continually until 1107. Now Turgot had to deal with the new king's agent when he came to claim the revenue from the bishop's estates.

To add to the prior's difficulties, King Henry I began taking over estates which were legitimately owned by the diocese. The revenues of three Yorkshire manors— Allertonshire (Northallerton), Welton and Howden—were diverted to the king until 1116. Land at Marske-by-the-Sea, which had been given to Cuthbert by Copsig,[79] agent of Earl Tostig, around 1065, was lost. During Flambard's absence Cumbria, with Hexhamshire and Teviotshire, was also appropriated from the bishopric of Durham and annexed to the archdeaconry of Richmond, in the diocese of York.[80] Similarly, Teviotdale was transferred from Durham to the diocese of Glasgow, which deprived the bishopric of revenues from Berwickshire.

During the interregnum, Turgot had continued with the building work, but the cost to the monks was more than financial: "The monks neglected the monastic buildings and concentrated on the construction of the church, which Ranulf consequently found built as far as the nave".[81] In Flambard's absence, Turgot continued the work on the new cathedral, completing the eastern arm, the crossing and the eastern side of the transepts by 1104.[82]

▶ *Durham Cathedral: part of the south transept in 1841, from Billings* PLATE L.

Ranulf Flambard

Flambard was the chief financial and legal agent of King William Rufus throughout his reign 1087–1100. The king and Flambard were of a similar disposition, each possessing ready wit and inventive skills, and neither having much time for religion. The king needed money and Flambard supplied it by acting through the royal administration. The surname 'Flambard', meaning 'devouring torch' or 'burning flame', was said to have been a nickname given him by Robert fitz Turstin, the Dispenser, about 1090, because of his consuming ambition.[83] Flambard saw a new opportunity to extract money from church estates when Archbishop Lanfranc died on 20 May 1089. When bishops or abbots died, the archbishop normally took charge of their estates until a new appointment was made. Now that the archbishop had died, such revenues from vacant sees and abbacies could be directed to the king. Thus from May 1089 until December 1093 Flambard and the king ensured that the archbishopric remained vacant so that the king could receive revenues from unfilled posts.

Even after a new prelate was appointed in 1093, when the king was ill and feared for his life, William Rufus continued to take a fee from his nominee. According to the annals of Winchester, Flambard had sixteen vacant bishoprics and abbacies under his care in 1097.[84] Each vacancy was worth about £250 a year and in 1097 provided about twenty percent of the king's annual revenue. Archbishop Anselm, writing to Pope Paschal II (1099–1118), remarked that Flambard was "not only a tax-gatherer but the most notorious chief of tax-gatherers".[85]

At Durham, which was vacant from 1096 to 1099, £300 per annum was taken from the bishopric to the royal treasury,[86] though the king took nothing from the monks. The capital value must have been over £1,500 and, with its high prestige and importance, was worth much more. In 1099 Flambard offered to purchase the bishopric of Durham for £1000, and was nominated to the bishopric by the king.[87] The appointment was made on Whitsunday 29 May in the first royal court held by William Rufus in his new hall at Westminster,[88] and Flambard was consecrated on 5 June at St Paul's Cathedral, London.[89] However, when he became bishop he lost his position as the king's right-hand man.

On 2 August 1100 William Rufus was killed while hunting. His younger brother Henry I claimed the throne and, just ten days after his coronation, the king sent Flambard to the Tower of London on 15 August to become the first state prisoner there. He was deprived of his bishopric after less than fifteen months.

Flambard had made many friends through his position and wealth, and they needed him to be available in the new political situation. They helped him to escape on 2 February 1101 by providing a feast for his guards, wine to make them drunk, rope smuggled in for the descent, horses to make his escape, and a ship to take him and his mother to Normandy. Trusted companions also brought his treasure.[90]

Normandy was a separate country from England at this time, where Robert Curthose, elder brother of Henry of England, ruled as duke. Robert welcomed the exiles, and Flambard was soon made chief adviser to the duke. He assisted in raising an army to invade England which set out on 20 July 1101.

The royal brothers met at Alton, Hampshire, with Flambard smoothing the way. Robert agreed to renounce any claim to the English throne in return for a pension of £2,000 from Henry. Flambard continued as a deviser and manager of schemes. He sought the indulgence of Henry I, suggesting that he could act for the good of England with his knowledge of affairs in the duchy. Duke Robert issued a charter of safe conduct for Flambard to return to England, and he was present at the royal council at Windsor on 3 September 1101,[91] but Henry never allowed him to wield power as he had been able to under William Rufus. Instead Henry found a supreme administrator of royal business in Roger, bishop of Salisbury. The king absolved Flambard of evil intent and reinstated him in 1103 as bishop of Durham, although Flambard appears to have continued to live in Normandy. The bishop began the slow process of reclaiming the lost possessions of his diocese, which had been quickly claimed by others.

From 1101 to 1106 Flambard was more active in Normandy than in England, supporting Duke Robert and being rewarded with the gift of the guardianship of the diocese of Lisieux. When the bishopric of Lisieux became vacant in August 1101, Flambard used his influence to secure the see for his brother Fulcher, who was consecrated in June 1102, but died soon after. Flambard then secured a long-term settlement that his own son Thomas should become bishop, with reversion to another son in the event of the death of the elder brother.[92] When Henry invaded Normandy in 1106, achieving victory at Tinchebrai on 28 September and capturing Duke Robert, Flambard sent messengers to the king offering him the town of Lisieux. Flambard remained involved at Lisieux until 1107, when John of Séez was appointed bishop there.

Flambard had his children some time before 1099, by Alveva (Ælfgifu), whose niece became the hermit, Christina of Markyate. He then married Alveva off to a townsman in Huntingdon. Even when made bishop of Durham he continued to lodge at their house on his journeys to and from Durham. On one such occasion, when Christina was about 16, the bishop had the girl brought to him in his chamber while the parents were drinking in the hall below. He took hold of Christina by one of the sleeves of her tunic and attempted to seduce her. The quick-witted girl thwarted his advances by suggesting that she bolted the door first. He agreed, but she bolted the door from the outside![93]

At the Council of Westminster in September 1125, called by the papal legate John of Crema, Flambard was accused of incontinence. Flambard invited the legate to his palace at Durham, and made his niece available to entertain his guest. At the most inopportune time, members of the bishop's household burst into the chamber and proffered gifts in celebration. John of Crema returned to Rome, but there was no censuring of Flambard for incontinence.[94]

About a month before he died, sitting facing the altar, "with only clerks and many men of the bishopric standing round him, he began ... to repent deeply of all the evil which he had committed against the church ... he restored to the church everything he had taken away, and confirmed these restitutions by his charter under his seal".[95]

Flambard died on 5 September 1128, aged about 68, after falling ill "at the beginning of the dog-days, and he died when they came to an end".[96] His grave, in the centre of the chapter house, was excavated in 1874.[97]

Symeon's continuator sums up the ambiguities of Flambard's personality:

" ... this bishop had in him a great spirit, which he had derived from the power he had enjoyed when he had formerly been procurator of the kingdom, so that in any gathering of great men he always strove to be either the first of them or to be amongst the first, and he obtained a magnificent place of honour amongst those who were honoured. With his immensely loud voice and his threatening looks, he simulated indignation rather than showing it in reality. With the eloquent inventiveness of his words, in which he mixed the jocular with the serious, he left his listeners in doubt as to what was true and what false. His mood was also sometimes capricious, so that neither his anger nor his merriment would last long, but he would change easily from one to the other".[98]

▲ *The head of Flambard's crosier, found in his tomb in 1874, from Fowler,* Excavations PLATE XXXI.

CHAPTER 4

Turgot the Servant of St Cuthbert

Turgot was devoted to St Cuthbert and his shrine. In his *Life of St Margaret Queen of Scotland* he describes himself as "servant of the servants of St Cuthbert".[1] But, to Turgot, Cuthbert was not just an historical figure from a distant past. He believed the saint to be still active on behalf of his servants.

As prior of Durham monastery, Turgot had to inspire and lead some forty monks to serve St Cuthbert daily at his shrine. The prior ensured that they believed in the power and the glory of the saint, just as they did in the Lord.

The miracles of St Cuthbert

Bede's *Life of St Cuthbert* in prose form, written around 721, records numerous miracles performed by the saint during his lifetime and immediately after his death. Further posthumous miracles attributed to the saint were recorded by the *congregatio* of St Cuthbert at Chester-le-Street in the mid-tenth century in a work known as *Historia de Sancto Cuthberto*. By about 1130 another collection of miracles had been compiled, known as *Liber de miraculis et translationibus sancti Cuthberti*. Twenty-one post-Bedan miracles credited to the saint's intervention are recorded.[2]

▲ *Durham Cathedral: site of St Cuthbert's shrine in 1841, from Billings* PLATE XXVIII.

In accepting Christianity, the Northumbrians would expect their new God to have powers no less spectacular than their former gods. Those converted by miracles were enthusiastic, but lacked knowledge of the traditions of the Church. Those who knew about the traditions sometimes lacked experience of miracles, and often found themselves dismissed as extremists. In the pre-scholastic age, miracles were the main arguments to establish truth. Miracles, signs and wonders were part of everyday living and, for the poor, helped to make life tolerable. Even modern man accepts, just as ignorantly, the manifestations of electronic wizardry. All men met on common ground, and regardless of class, could accept miracles. The manifestations of each miracle testified to the displeasure as well as the power of the saint. The chief miracle of St Cuthbert was the continuing preservation of his body from decay.

The first seven miracles took place before the monastery at Durham was founded. These dealt with persons who interfered with the saint's property and were duly punished.

In the eighth to the seventeenth, and the twenty-first, miracles the sinners are pardoned and restored, mostly through the mediation of the prior. These reveal actions of Turgot more in line with New Testament standards. No biography of Turgot would be complete without knowledge of his part in these miracles. Many of the monks were eyewitnesses.

The eighteenth, nineteenth and twentieth miracles refer to the translation of the incorrupt body of St Cuthbert to a new shrine in 1104. The bishop took no part in the preparations, which were initiated entirely by the prior.

The miracle accounts were probably not written by Turgot, for it was unlikely that he would praise his own liberality and humanity. But he would have ensured that the miracles in which he had been involved were known to all, to the praise of St Cuthbert, but also to the praise of the God whom he and Cuthbert both served.

Other stories survive of St Cuthbert's intervention, such as William I's uncomfortable visit to Durham in 1072,[3] and the appearance of the saint to Ralph, the king's tax collector, chiding him for unjustly taxing his flock and warning of punishment if he continued.[4]

Miracles of St Cuthbert

The post-Bedan miracles divide into four groups:

- **Miracles 1 to 7:** written by a Durham monk soon after the monastery was founded in 1083. The last miracle cited took place in 1080. There is much use of alliteration and rhetorical questions.
- **Miracles 8 to 17:** written around 1100 to 1115 with a simpler style of writing. The presence of Turgot the prior in miracles 10 to 17 is always significant. He is seldom mentioned by name but in miracle 10 as "*praepositus monasterii*" (prior of the monastery) and in 11 as "*praepositus memoratus*" (renowned prior). Miracles 11 to 17 reveal the new priory in existence, with Turgot in charge. He is shown to be full of active concern for everyone he encountered.

- **Miracles 18 to 20:** written about 1125, or even after Flambard's death in 1128. The reference to Ralph of Séez as "a man of venerable memory" indicates that this account was written after his death on 19 September 1122. Prior Turgot had also died and the author of these miracles had been present at the translation of St Cuthbert in 1104. He was deeply impressed by every happening. F. M. Powicke suggested that Maurice, abbot of Rievaulx (1145–7), may have been the author, as a book by him on the translation of St Cuthbert is listed in a thirteenth-century catalogue of manuscripts at Rievaulx. He was brought up at Durham from youth and became sub-prior in 1138, leaving soon after to become a Cistercian at Rievaulx.[5] Miracles 18 to 20 together with miracle 21 form the 'translation group' of 1104.
- **Miracle 21:** This mentions "*memoratus prior*" and was probably written about 1105.

Miracle 1: 877–8 Glastonbury marshes
St Cuthbert appears to King Alfred in a vision. Cuthbert, appearing as a pilgrim, had been treated kindly by the king and the saint promises victory over the Danes.[6]

Miracle 2: c.882 Cumbria and Crayke, Yorkshire
The body of the saint is transported from Lindisfarne by the *congregatio*, with the intention of taking it to Ireland. A great tempest and three waves of blood drive the ship back to shore. The saint is taken to Crayke and on to Chester-le-Street.[7]

Miracle 3: before 915 Chester-le-Street
St Cuthbert's lands are divided by the Vikings and given to Scula and Onlafbald. The latter enters Cuthbert's church at Chester-le-Street and mocks the saint. He is struck down, seeks pardon, but dies in agony.[8]

Miracle 4: c.890 near Chester-le-Street
The Scots army attacks Lindisfarne and crosses the Tyne, threatening Cuthbert's shrine at Chester-le-Street. Through the intervention of the saint the "ground opened up and swallowed the Scots alive".[9]

Miracle 5: c.1060 Durham
Tostig, earl of Northumbria, imprisons a robber, but Cuthbert frees him of his chains. He seeks sanctuary in Durham Cathedral and is pursued by one of Tostig's men, Barcwith, who attempts to secure the robber. The pursuer collapses and suffers for three days before dying. Tostig befriends the robber, Aldan-hamal, and everyone contributes to providing the church with a fine cross and a Gospel book decorated with gold and precious stones.[10]

Miracle 6: 1069 Lindisfarne
William the Norman takes vengeance for the murder of Robert de Comines, earl of Northumbria, in 1068. The body of St Cuthbert is removed for safety to Lindisfarne but on arrival the *congregatio* find it is high tide with the causeway under water. The sea parts and allows them to pass dry-shod to the island.[11]

Miracle 7: 1080 Durham
A Norman soldier at Durham Castle enters the cathedral intent on stealing treasure which he had noticed. He suffers a burning fever and dies in torment, in spite of confessing his ill deeds.[12]

Miracle 8: between 1087 and 1100 near Durham
A man attends Durham Fair on St Cuthbert's Day (4 September) allowing his horse to feed on a corn-stack in a field belonging to the monastery. The horse dies and the man goes barefoot to Cuthbert's shrine. The monks are present and the man is pardoned.[13]

Miracle 9: 1091 near Durham
The king of Scotland raids England and the "people of Cuthbert" and others flock into Durham for safety. The crowds are stifled by the summer heat and suffer intolerable conditions. William Rufus sends an army north and the advance of Malcolm is halted not far from the city. St Cuthbert intervenes and both armies retire. There is mention of the prior, and of the bishop's return from exile.[14]

Miracle 10: after 1091 England to the south
Prior Turgot journeys south in winter-time with two of the brethren to attend the royal court on behalf of the *haliwerfolc* (the people of the saint). Supporters accompany them, but when they attempt to find accommodation in a certain village, they are rejected. One householder mocks the monks and their saint, resulting in the villager's collapse "as if dead". By the intervention of St Cuthbert and the request of the monks, he is restored to life. News of the event was enjoyed at the king's court.[15]

Miracle 11: after 1091 Lindisfarne
Prior Turgot and brethren find a shoal of sixty-five great fish washed up on the shore but are refused their share as it was not on their property. They wander, distressed that Lent had ended and they were without food. Suddenly they find another stranded shoal of sixty-seven even larger fish and on part of the shore which belonged to the monastery. The additional fare enhanced Easter rejoicings.[16]

Miracle 12: 1093 Tynemouth
Robert de Mowbray, earl of Northumbria (1081–95), gives the church at Tynemouth to St Albans Abbey. This belonged to Durham, and Abbot Paul of St Albans is taken ill and dies when he arrives to claim Cuthbert's property.[17]

Miracle 13: before 1100 Durham

A clerk from the south suffers a chronic fever. He spends a night at Cuthbert's shrine witnessed by "fellow monks", after which he is healed.[18]

Miracle 14: before 1100 Durham

The belt of the stable-lad of the monastery is stolen by a known thief, who refuses to return it. The boy appeals to Cuthbert and the thief becomes blind. The thief makes his confession to the saint, restores the belt to its owner, and his blindness is partially cured.[19]

Miracle 15: before 1100 Lindisfarne

A horse is stolen from the monastery and when the thief crosses the causeway to the mainland the tide rises miraculously and he fears drowning. He calls for help from the saint who allows him to return. The stolen horse is retrieved and the repentant thief is allowed to walk back to the mainland.[20]

Miracle 16: ?1094/5 near Durham

Eight bullocks are transporting a huge log up a hill towards Durham when a child falls with his leg seemingly crushed beneath the beam. Sixteen men were needed to lift the log and release the child. He was found unhurt.[21]

Miracle 17: c.1102 Lindisfarne

Pirates seize one of the monastery's trading ships off the coast, and the crew are put ashore. Later the pirates' own ship is driven ashore by storm. Prior Turgot treats them kindly not knowing that they are pirates. The crew of the monastic vessel regain possession and sail into harbour, recognise the pirates, and urge the prior to execute them. Turgot spares them and arranges for their accommodation. On their departure the pirate ship is given to the monastery.[22]

Miracle 18: 1104 Durham

This is an account of the opening of the coffin of the saint by the prior and nine monks on 24 August. The doubts of an abbot lead to the second examination of the body by four abbots and other clergy. The translation is performed on 29 August when the bishop's sermon is ended by a miraculous heavy shower of rain.[23]

Miracle 19: 1104 Durham

Richard d'Aubigny, abbot of St Albans, is asked by Prior Turgot to assist in placing the coffin on a specially made slab supported on nine pillars, at the new shrine. As the abbot touches the coffin he is healed of a long-standing infirmity of his left hand.[24]

Miracle 20: 1104 Durham

During his long sermon at the translation, Bishop Ranulf shows the people a relic of Cuthbert's own copy of St John's Gospel. It was enclosed in a leather satchel with a silken band, much frayed, by which it was hung round the neck, first of Boisil and then of Cuthbert (see pp. 3–5). One of Flambard's officials removes a thread and hides it in his shoe, but on the following night he suffers a severe pain and a swollen leg. He confesses his guilt and limps with a stick to Prior Turgot and offers the silken thread. The prior insists that it must be returned personally to the saint, but the man fears to go alone. Some of the brethren accompany him, and the man prays at the shrine and is restored to perfect health.[25]

Miracle 21: *c.*1105 Durham

A new great bell is cast in London on the orders of Turgot, which requires a specially constructed wagon for its transport to Durham, drawn by twenty-two bullocks. A youth is caught up by his garment and dragged to the ground. The wheels pass over him crushing his loins, shoulder and an arm, and he "lay motionless as if dead". The monk in charge prays to St Cuthbert and gradually the youth recovers, remarking that the bell is heavy. Little by little he begins to walk with the aid of a stick until he finally arrives at Durham. The youth immediately goes to the shrine of the saint to give thanks.[26]

The translation of St Cuthbert

The late sixteenth-century text, *Rites of Durham*, records the tradition that, during the years of rebuilding, St Cuthbert's shrine had been housed "in ye cloister garth over against ye parloure dour",[27] possibly in a part of the old cathedral building that had escaped demolition. By August 1104 the eastern arm of the new cathedral was complete, ready to receive its saint, and plans were put in place for the shrine to be translated to its new position.

Although Bishop Ranulf Flambard had effected a reconciliation with Henry I in 1101, he continued to spend most of his time in Normandy until 1107. He made a brief visit to England late in September 1102 to observe the building progress of Durham Cathedral. His restitution as bishop was agreed and absolution given by Archbishop Anselm. He began to retrieve his widespread estates from those occupying them—a task which would take three years. So, from the illness of William of St-Calais in 1095 until the translation of St Cuthbert in 1104, Prior Turgot had been responsible for the construction and fitting out of the new cathedral. This would have involved altar furnishings, choir-stalls, woodcarvings, statues, chandeliers, candelabra, general decorating and ordering of services. However, the bishop made sure he was in Durham for the translation ceremony of St Cuthbert into the new cathedral. He would have wanted to make the most of such a public spectacle as the veneration of an important saint, staged amid dazzling architecture.

29 August 1104 was a momentous day at Durham, when the body of St Cuthbert was translated to a new shrine in the eastern apse of the cathedral. William of Malmesbury (*c.*1125) relates a strange happening a few days before the translation took place, when St Cuthbert himself removed the timber centring which supported the vault of the presbytery.[28] This informs us that this was vaulted—the first use of vaulted ribs over a high and wide span. The internal width of the apse was 31 feet (9.5m).

Invitations were sent out to the nobility and clergy, near and far, to attend the ceremony, and as the guests began arriving, there was murmuring about the claims of the monks with regard to the legend of St Cuthbert, including the incorruption of his body. The claim rested, some said, on the faith of tradition. The passage of four centuries made it impossible that the body could remain in the same state as at the time of Bede. Disregarding the passage of time, but taking into account the devastations by the Danes, the vicissitudes of subsequent journeys and the negligence of attendants, the saint could not be entire, and many visitors wondered if Durham possessed even Cuthbert's ashes.

These reports alarmed the Durham monks, especially when Bishop Ranulf arrived and voiced his scepticism. Those who affirmed that the body was in a perfect state became anxious and ashamed. The Durham community had to demonstrate their faith in the incorruptible state of their saint, so Turgot summoned the monks to a meeting in the chapter house. No doubt he would have recounted to them his experiences in Norway and the well-known story of King Magnus the Good, son of St Olav, who in the years 1042–46 opened the sarcophagus of his father every year, in order to trim the beard and cut the nails of his father (see p. 15).[29]

Turgot opens the tomb

After a long and solemn consultation it was decided that Turgot the prior, with nine brothers, should open the tomb and make a faithful report concerning the state of its contents.[30] Reginald names them as the sub-prior Aldwine, Leofwine, Wilking, Godwin, and Osbern, the sacristans, Henry and William surnamed Havegrin, both archdeacons, Algar, afterwards prior (1109–1137), and Symeon (the chronicler).[31]

There is an anonymous account of the opening of the tomb, which is thought to have been composed c.1123 by an eyewitness of the event, but not Symeon.[32] This can be supplemented by information that Reginald of Durham claimed he had been told by "the elder brethren of our church. They, truly, have seen and heard those who handled the incorruptible body of St Cuthbert . . . and from them our brethren have learned the more intimate facts about it".[33] On 24 August 1104, as soon as their brethren were retired to rest, Turgot and the nine monks, having fasted and prayed, "prostrated themselves before the venerable coffin, and amid tears and prayers they laid hands upon it, not without fear and trembling, to open it. Aided by instruments of iron, they soon succeeded in their attempt, when, to their astonishment, they found a chest covered on all sides with hides, diligently prepared and fixed to it by iron nails." Overcoming their initial fears, "they renewed their task, and having succeeded in opening the iron bands, they lifted up the lid. Here they saw within, a coffin of wood, which had been covered all over by coarse linen cloth of a threefold texture, of the length of a man, and covered with a lid of the same description".[34] Reginald tells us this cloth, "which surrounded and enclosed the coffin" had been "entirely impregnated with wax", and the anonymous author later mentions a linen cover "dipped in wax".[35] Encouraged by Leofwine, "the brethren regained their confidence by this admonition of a devout servant of God and moved the venerable body from behind the altar, where it had hitherto reposed, into the middle of the choir—a place more spacious and better adapted to the investigation".[36] They removed the lid of the coffin and, by candlelight, saw a copy of the Gospels, on a wide shelf which covered the body. By the help of two iron rings, fixed on the extremities, it was easily removed. The prior encouraged them as they "smelt an odour of the sweetest fragrancy"[37] and disclosed the body lying on its right side, apparently entire.

At the sight they gazed on each other in silent astonishment; and "shrank back to some distance, not daring to look at the miracle before their eyes . . . Whilst they were in this state, each related to the one who was nearest to him what he had seen, just as if he had been the only one favoured with the sight".[38] Still some distance from the coffin, the monks repeated in a low voice the seven psalms of penitence, and then approached on their hands and knees.[39]

Gradually their fears were dispelled; they arose, and approached the coffin, and three of them, by order of the prior, placing hands under the head (Reginald names him as Osbern the sacrist), the feet (Aldwine the sub-prior), and the middle of the body (Algar, later prior), raised it up, and laid it respectfully on "tapestry and other robes" spread on the floor.[40]

In the coffin they found a great number of bones within separate linen bags, the mortal remains of other bishops of Lindisfarne. Cuthbert had been laid on his side in order to provide room for the bones of these and other saints. These were removed and transferred to a different part of the church, so that they could lay the saint upon his back, and place between his hands the head of St Oswald, who had been martyred in 642 at Oswestry.[41] As the hour of matins approached, they hastily replaced the body in the coffin, and carried it back to its former situation.[42]

▲ *The discovery of St Cuthbert's incorrupt body in 1104. Drawing by Rosemary Turner, based on Oxford, University College MS 165 folio 118r.*

At the chapter meeting in the morning, the full assembly of monks were informed of the discoveries. Bishop Ranulf, briefly present at Durham, refused to believe their report and declared that even a sworn statement would scarcely satisfy him.

The following night, the same monks again carried the saint's body into the choir and placed it upon vestments spread on the pavement. They discovered that it had been dressed in "a robe of a costly kind, next below this it was wrapped in a purple dalmatic, and then in linen, and all these were whole and fair, and retained their original freshness without any stain of corruption".[43] With it had been buried a pair of scissors, a comb of ivory, a silver altar, a paten, and a small chalice. "By examining it with their eyes, by handling it with their hands, by raising it and lowering it, they had clearly discovered that it was a body in a state of incorruption, with solid sinews . . . they clothed it with the most costly pall . . . and restored it to the place behind the altar where it had formerly rested".[44]

The following morning the monks were eager to announce the discovery of the preceding night, and a solemn act of thanksgiving was performed, to publish their triumph, and silence the doubts of the incredulous.

"In the mean while, the day of the approaching translation being made known far and wide, there was a great flocking to Durham from every side. Men of all ranks, ages and professions, the secular and the spiritual, all hastened to be present. They had heard of the miracle, that the body, although dead for so many years, was still free from decay . . . and they gloried in the fact that such a wonder was made manifest in their time".[45] But their joy was soon interrupted when the abbot of a neighbouring monastery asked why darkness was selected as the most proper time to visit the tomb, and none but the monks of Durham were permitted to be present. This had been undertaken without consulting him, or allowing him to share the proceedings. Many had assembled for the occasion and all had to be satisfied about the facts. He considered that the monks were unworthy of belief, so he repeatedly asked that the coffin be opened before the eyes of the strangers who had come to assist at the translation of the relics. This unexpected demand, with the insinuations by which it was accompanied, roused the indignation of the monks.[46]

The altercation continued till 29 August, the day appointed for the ceremony of the translation, when the abbot of Séez prevailed on Prior Turgot to accede to so reasonable a demand. Ralph d'Escures, abbot of Séez in Normandy (1089–1108), and bishop elect of Rochester,[47] was probably attending as the representative of the king, who had left England earlier in the month on his first visit to Normandy since his accession.[48] The abbot felt that any doubt had to be removed, and further examination would result in greater glory for the church of Durham and, as those present returned home, the glory of St Cuthbert would spread to all the world.[49]

The monks of Durham still feared judgement from above if they exposed the holy body to view, but Turgot agreed that a certain number of fit persons, including the abbots, should be admitted to see the miracle. To the number of fifty they entered the choir, led by Prior Turgot, followed by the abbot of Séez, Richard d'Aubigny, abbot of St Albans (1096–1119), Stephen, abbot of St Mary, York (1085–1112), Hugh de Lacy, abbot of St Germans, Selby (1097–1123), Alexander, brother and heir of Edgar, king of the Scots, and the bishop's chaplain, William de Corbeil.[50] The bishop of Durham was not present as he was dedicating an altar in the cathedral.[51]

The chest which enclosed the remains was placed before them, and the lid was removed. Turgot stepped forward and, stretching out his hand, forbade any person to touch the body without his permission, and commanded his monks to ensure the execution of his orders. He asked those present to acquaint themselves with the truth with their eyes and not their hands—nothing must be removed from the coffin—and all obeyed. The abbot of Séez then approached and proved the flexibility of the joints, by moving the head, the arms, and the legs. He pulled an ear "in no gentle manner" and felt other parts of the body and found "solid sinews and bones, and clothed with the softness of flesh". The abbot exclaimed, "My brethren, the body which we have before us is unquestionably dead, but it is just as sound and entire as when it was forsaken by its holy soul on its way to the skies." At the sight every doubt vanished; the most incredulous confessed that they were satisfied; the *Te Deum* was chanted, and the translation of the relics to the sanctuary of the new cathedral was immediately performed with the accustomed ceremonies.[52]

St Cuthbert's tomb opened again

The tomb has been opened at least three times since 1104. In 1539 Henry VIII's commissioners stripped the gold, silver and jewels from the shrine but, on opening the coffin, discovered a body "hole and incorrupted", dressed in priestly vestments "freshe saife & not consumed".[53] It was therefore left alone and later re-interred. The grave was opened again in 1827, revealing a complete skeleton still clothed in fragments of the ancient vestments.[54] The skeleton and other human relics were placed in a new coffin and returned to the grave, but the remains of the seventh-century coffin, the fragments of vestments and other ancient artefacts were removed. Drawings made by the cathedral librarian, James Raine, are reproduced on the following pages.[55] The original items are now on display at the cathedral. The grave was also opened in 1899, when the body was anatomically examined before being re-interred.[56]

▲ *The gold cross.*

▲ *Inscriptions on the coffin.*

▲ ▶ *Two sections of the
tenth-century stole.*

◀ *The tenth-century
girdle or 'small maniple'.*

◀ ▲ *The ends of the
tenth-century maniple.*

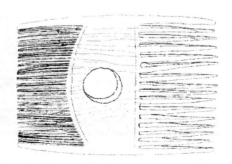

◀ *The silver altar.*   ▲ *The ivory comb.*

◀ *The seventh-century "Nature Goddess Silk".*

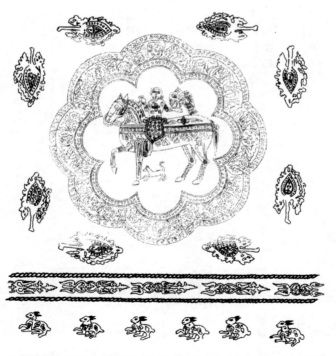

◀ *The tenth- or early eleventh-century "Rider Silk".*

A new shrine for St Cuthbert

Those waiting outside burst into tears of joy, and fell flat to the ground. The procession with the coffin of Cuthbert perambulated around the new church with difficulty because of the crowds. Bishop Ranulf preached a sermon on resurrection, proclaiming the incorruption of Cuthbert's body, which, after 418 years was yet flexible and immortal. Aloft for all to see he held Cuthbert's copy of St John's Gospel. For monkish tastes, Ranulf's sermon was largely irrelevant and far too long. The brightness of the day had been such that there was no sign of bad weather, when suddenly torrents of rain began to fall. The brethren, interrupting the sermon, snatched up the coffin of the saint and hastily conveyed it into the new church, whereupon the rain ceased.[57]

William of Malmesbury (c.1125) suggests that the storm was Cuthbert's displeasure at being turned into a spectacle. "There was a long procession of people going and coming back, and a great crush where people jostled at the front, for having once seen the body they wanted to see it again and again. A sudden heavy storm drove everybody into the half-completed church. And it was miraculous that although the monks had been drenched by the force of the storm, their garments were not only undamaged, but not even made wet".[58]

"At length, the body of the blessed pontiff having been decently restored to its place, a solemn mass was performed, whilst all the while the church was echoing with peals of praise, and the mysteries for the safety of the faithful being gone through, all returned home with joy, glorifying and praising God for what they had seen and heard".[59] Reference to the "church . . . echoing with peals of praise" suggests a completed vault and not the coarse fabric of a temporary roof.

In preparation for the ceremony, a sub-structure of stone had been built behind the high altar of the new cathedral. Alexander of Scotland was privileged to be present at the translation as he "gave many marks of gold and silver, and caused to be prepared a shrine in which the sacred body, enveloped in new vestments, was honourably preserved".[60] The reliquary-coffin of the incorrupt body was to be lifted up higher behind the altar.[61] There were at least two steps to the platform,[62] on which nine columns supported a finely decorated marble slab bearing the coffin. From recorded miracles, we learn that pilgrims were able to crawl between the columns which were about three feet (1 metre) in height.[63] There was an altar on the west side of the shrine, at which mass was to be said on St Cuthbert's day.[64]

At the ceremony of the translation, Prior Turgot decided to make a last minute adjustment to the coffin, and climbed onto the marble slab. He invited abbot Richard d'Aubigny of St Albans to help him, but the abbot had a paralysed left hand. He joined Turgot and immediately his hand was cured.[65] A member of the bishop's household removed a silken thread from the ties of the leather bag containing St John's Gospel, but Turgot ordered him to restore it to St Cuthbert.[66]

Illustrations of the shrine appear in a few copies of Bede's *Life of St Cuthbert*, but they may be an imaginary conception.[67] A window in Trinity Chapel, Canterbury, shows a similar shrine for Becket. Cuthbert's shrine and its fame endured for the next 435 years, until the Reformation, 852 years after Cuthbert's death. (The shrine was destroyed by Henry VIII's commissioners, and the body buried beneath the paving behind the High Altar.)

▲ *The shrine of St Cuthbert, of marble and gold, with an enormous emerald.*[68] *Drawing by Rosemary Turner, based on Oxford, University College MS 165 folio 130r.*

▼ *A sick man is cured at Cuthbert's tomb. Drawing by Rosemary Turner, based on Oxford, University College MS 165 folio 122r.*

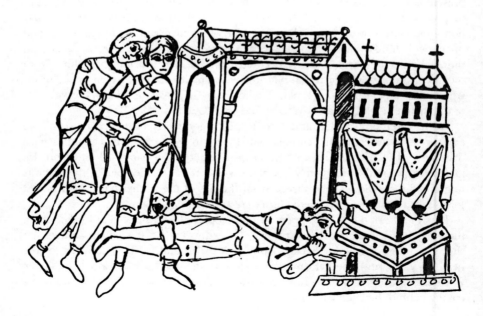

▲ *Barcwith who invaded Cuthbert's sanctuary is struck down (see miracle 5). Drawing by Rosemary Turner, based on Oxford, University College MS 165 folio 157r.*

▼ *A Norman thief who stole from St Cuthbert's shrine is struck dead (see miracle 7). Drawing by Rosemary Turner, based on Oxford, University College MS 165 folio 163r.*

The esteem for Prior Turgot must have risen to new heights after the new cathedral came into use. Not only did the building contain many innovations in construction and decoration, but the body of St Cuthbert had been translated to its new resting place, and Turgot had seen the miracle of the incorrupt body. Turgot had seen the face of Cuthbert. Even the bishop had not done this. This must have impressed all who subsequently met the prior. The translation in 1104 was the biggest coup for Durham.

The existence of the new shrine would have increased the offerings from pilgrims and benefactors, enabling work to continue on the north transept roof and the eastern bays of the nave. Turgot remained in charge of the construction until Flambard's return in 1107.

Flambard's return

Ranulf Flambard went back to Normandy after the ceremony. He visited England again in 1105,[69] but it was not until 1107 that he finally returned to England. In May he was at Winchester witnessing a charter of Henry's queen, Matilda.[70] Flambard was not fully operative as bishop until 1112, when a series of bishop's *acta* began. There are no known manuscripts issued under his episcopacy before 1122.[71] Bishop Ranulf had a well-organised episcopal household which attracted scholars and administrators, who lived in the palace within the castle. One was his chaplain, William de Corbeil, who became archbishop of Canterbury in the bishop's lifetime.

The monastic community, led by the formidable Turgot, posed a considerable obstacle to the free exercise of Flambard's authority. Gerard, archbishop of York (1100–08), had written to Turgot and the monks, advising them to receive the bishop on his return from exile "with reverence as lord and father, and obey him in all things as good sons".[72]

The long experience of 'self-rule' by Durham monastery meant that, when Flambard finally took up residence in his palace, he encountered a community used to controlling the duties and needs of the diocese. Turgot had to resist the encroachments of Flambard upon the possessions and privileges of the monks. The bishop ignored the financial arrangements agreed with the previous bishop in 1091/92, diverting the altar dues and burial fees from monastic needs and using them to pay for the completion of the nave of the cathedral. The bishop "acted at times more assiduously and at others with more remissness, depending on whether offerings made at the altar or dues from the cemetery were available to him or lacking".[73] He completed the nave walls up to the vaulting.

In spite of being the titular abbot of Durham monastery, Flambard was not a monk and could take no part in the daily routine. In fact, there were parts of the precinct which he could not visit without permission. The monastery had become a powerful institution in the community and the bishop was having to resist the cult of St Cuthbert which, through the merits of the saint and miraculous episodes, dominated the monks' lives.

Flambard's desire to build, particularly in the town of Durham, continued. He was "so impatient of leisure that he moved on from task to task, thinking nothing of what he had achieved, concerned only that new tasks should take the place of those already accomplished".[74]

When Turgot was chosen to be bishop of St Andrews in 1108,[75] Flambard was fully in favour. Turgot had been a major obstacle to his ambitions to benefit himself and his family at the expense of the church of St Cuthbert. Turgot could not be consecrated until Thomas, archbishop-elect of York, had himself been consecrated. Flambard sent a special messenger to Anselm, archbishop of Canterbury, proposing to consecrate Turgot as bishop "by himself in the presence of the archbishop elect of York, associating with himself for that purpose the bishops of Scotland and the Orkneys".[76] When Anselm heard of the request he commented on the unseemly haste in expediting Turgot's promotion,[77] and replied that this would be uncanonical as Turgot must be consecrated by the archbishop of York. Thomas was consecrated on 27 June 1109, and Turgot's consecration followed on 1 August.[78]

Turgot had achieved his high ambitions for Durham Cathedral. The new building was not yet finished, but completion was now in prospect. The offer of a bishopric was not one he could refuse, and it was obvious that his relationship with Flambard would not improve. He had served St Cuthbert as well as he could, and now he would serve the greater Church, with the promise of being "seated with Him in heavenly realms".[79]

It is not clear whether Turgot had to give up his position as prior of Durham on his appointment to St Andrews, but Flambard lost no time in making his nephew Ranulf the new archdeacon. This was contrary to the constitutions of Bishop William of St-Calais, which laid down that the holder of the priorate must always be archdeacon. Flambard's son Osbert was appointed sheriff of Durham and Norham upon Tweed.

The cathedral is completed

The high vault of the north transept at Durham had now been completed. This is probably the earliest surviving example of a roof with diagonal ribs.[80] When Flambard first arrived at Durham he found the church "built as far as the nave".[81]

Like Turgot, Flambard was a builder. From 1104 to 1110 he was rebuilding in the latest fashion Christchurch Priory, formerly called Twinham, Hampshire (now Dorset), having demolished the old minster church in 1098.[82] There he built the nave, transepts and apsidal chapels, but the roof above the triforium was built by his successor.[83] Like many wealthy men, Flambard wished to build, to make a lasting memorial of his presence.

Flambard completed the walls and arcade of the nave at Durham in a similar manner to Christchurch.[84] Every alternate pier consists of a cylindrical column, each being ornamented with zigzag chasings, reticulated work and other Norman devices. He also built the arches and piers in the triforium, anticipating stone groining of the roof. This was the same design that he used at Christchurch (see description on p. 75 and illustrations on pp. 64–5, 76).

The nave vaulting was completed after Flambard's death in 1128,[85] when the pointed style of architecture became prevalent. The position of the springing of the groined roof is unusual as the vaulting springs some feet lower than the floor of the clerestory itself.[86]

As with many tyrants, there will be some plaudits to record in the life of Bishop Ranulf Flambard, as well as numerous faults. With, no doubt, a little persuasion from the prior, Flambard improved the accommodation of the monks. He extended the cramped precinct, both in length and breadth.[87] He increased the endowments for the monastery, and provided rich vestments. Always the builder, he constructed a wall between the cathedral and the bishop's castle, and later, in 1121, he built the Framwellgate bridge across the river Wear.[88]

▲ *Durham Cathedral: the transepts looking north in 1841, from Billings* PLATE XLIX.

CHAPTER 5

Turgot the Builder

While it is right to pay homage to Bishop William of St-Calais for his vision and inspiration in initiating the creation of Durham Cathedral, and to Bishop Ranulf Flambard, whose energy and determination brought it near to completion, it is clear that their many absences, whether on matters of state or because of royal displeasure, prevented them from overseeing much of the work at first hand. That task inevitably fell to their prior, Turgot, whose experiences in Norway had no doubt equipped him well for such a task. During the interregnum following the death of Bishop William, Turgot and his monks had full responsibility for the work. Durham Cathedral is universally acknowledged to be a masterpiece of construction, exhibiting a high degree of perfection, due to the ingenious hands of its workmen. Built on an immense scale, it was a heroic achievement by the monks and their architect.

In 1866 the Revd J. H. Blunt informed the British Archaeological Association that "The greater portion of the Cathedral of Durham, as it now stands, was built between the years 1093 and 1130 . . . For about fifty years the mediaeval masons were at work, under some architect whose name neither he nor any one else thought it worth while to record, in building a structure which remains to this day as a monument of artistic taste and mechanical skill".[1] By 1922 John Bilson had established the detailed chronology of the building and concluded that "It was planned by a master of exceptional ability as a completely [stone] vaulted church, and its earliest ribbed vaults, over the eastern bays of the choir aisles, must have been built by 1096".[2]

Significant aspects of the plan of Durham Cathedral (p. 58) included an apsed east end, transepts without western aisles, a nave of eight bays, and a western doorway to the cloister. The eastern arm of Durham consists of four bays, whilst only two bays were normally built in cathedrals in Normandy. The transepts at Durham are of great length, being 190 feet (58m) externally, which is the same length as the eastern arm plus the crossing.

Several features had already made an appearance elsewhere:

- Roll mouldings: already present at York Minster and St Mary's York from 1089.
- Use of paired shafts with complete plinths: already used in Anglo-Saxon architecture.
- Windows with double-splays: already used in Anglo-Saxon architecture.
- Block-like plinths to pillars in the presbytery arcade with single upper chamfers: similar to the pillars at the base of the tower at Lastingham (1078–85) and at Tynemouth.
- Pillars with cushion capitals with small volutes in corners: similar to those in the square presbytery and the crypt at Lastingham (1078–85).
- The crossing responds of the presbytery and transept aisles consist of a "half-shaft against a dosseret[3] with flanking half-shafts":[4] similar to the responds in the crypt-aisles of Lastingham (1078–85), and created from a single block of stone.

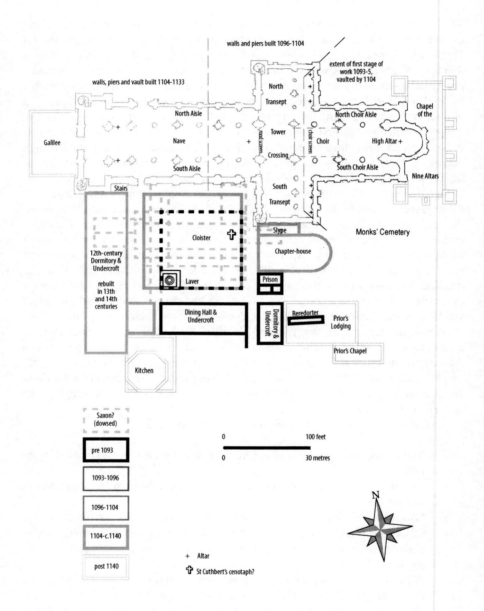

▲ *Plan of Turgot's cathedral and the twelfth-century claustral layout,*
based on VCH III facing p. 136, Bony, Stonework p. 21, Russo p.
260, Markuson p. 38 & Briggs, Cambridge & Bailey p. 96.

- Trumpet-cushion capitals above the dado of interlacing arcades in the presbytery aisles: similar to the west piers of the crossing at Lastingham (1078–85).
- Blind arcades on the walls of the slype and chapter house: similar to those in the crypt at Lastingham (1078–85).[5]

▲ *Durham Cathedral: innovative features in the choir, detail from Billings* PLATE XI.

However there were many innovations at Durham. Did Turgot and his colleagues realise that they were creating "a testing ground for a succession of unpredictable developments"?[6] They were prepared to take the risk of leading Western Europe in architectural experiment. Durham became a home of much novelty and of great significance:

1. Exterior wall arcading of the presbytery and transepts: exterior wall arcading was unknown in England in 1093. It is supported by two orders, which would have required extra centring for building each arch.
2. Interlacing dado arcading: this linear decoration appears along the interior walls of the presbytery. The arches have mouldings.
3. Massive plinths: the exterior bases are 5 feet (1.5m). The interior bases above floor level are 3 feet 3 inches (1m).
4. Columnar piers with octagonal capitals: though unknown in Normandy, cushion capitals were common in Germany, and subsequently appeared at Dunfermline, Kirkby Lonsdale, Kirkwall, Selby and Tynemouth.
5. Spiral decoration on columns with a diameter of 6 feet 6 inches (2m) to set off the shrine containing the relics, the first such columns in Norman England.
6. Alternating compound and cylindrical piers: this design was subsequently introduced at Lindisfarne.
7. Significant incised decoration on piers involving intricate masonry aligning each layer of stonework: this concept was subsequently introduced at Lindisfarne.

8. Earliest use of dressed stones of standard size and shape in making the incised cylindrical piers: a cost-effective method of assembling masonry pillars, involving fewer templates and faster construction.[7]
9. Neat joints in presbytery columns only 1.4 inches (35mm) thick: not adopted by most masons until the twelfth century. Winchester used rough joints until after 1107.[8]
10. Soffit-roll moulding in presbytery arcade: the first appearance in England, it heralded a new era in English church decoration. It appears on the continent from 1030–40 at Auxerre and Bernay, and was subsequently introduced at Lindisfarne.
11. Rib-vaults in eastern arm: Durham has the first high rib-vaults in Europe. These provided a skeleton to hold the cells of the body. This innovation was essential in the evolution of the gothic style of building. Subsequently introduced at Lindisfarne.
12. Use of corbels to support rib-vaults and vault shafts: subsequently introduced at Lindisfarne.
13. Chevron and zigzag decoration on arches, arch moulding and blind arcading: heralding a new era in decoration, subsequently introduced at Lindisfarne.
14. Large windows: more glazing, giving not only more light but more decoration.
15. The outer walls of the nave tied to the upper part of the main walls, the triforium, with half-arches of stone, strengthening the whole structure.

Such innovations were not sudden but progressive. Some ideas contained in early building campaigns, such as the rib-vaulting, were not fully developed until many years later.

▼ *Durham Cathedral: section—west side of the transepts, from Billings* PLATE XV.

Interlaced Arcading

Triforium

The master mason and his staff

We know little of the organisation of building work in the late eleventh or the twelfth centuries, but from the beginning of the thirteenth century much more information is available.

Masons held a monopoly of skills, which they guarded jealously. Each mason learned what was traditional in his lodge. Father taught son the methods of setting out, as well as certain geometrical and numerical formulae. By the thirteenth century the craft organisation exercised strict supervision of its members. A mason would progress through the stages of apprentice and journeyman before becoming a master. Apprenticeship lasted from five to seven years and involved carpentry and stone-carving, as well as the study of the geometry necessary for design.

Euclid's *Elements of Geometry* was not introduced into England until about 1120, in a translation by Adelard of Bath from an Arabic version, but it was not necessary for the mason to understand the theoretical basis of any design. He was able to manipulate basic figures such as the square, circle and triangle to produce lines and points from which any structure could evolve. Numerical ratios such as $1:\sqrt{2}$—the relationship of the side of a square to its diagonal—were used in a proportional system. Proportions were used to ensure structural stability.

The master mason had full control over the design of the templates, prepared by the carpenter, from which were cut the mouldings to be used on column bases, voussoirs of arches, and tracery for arcades and windows. Templates were also produced for ribs, pier patterns, windows, etc. The master mason determined all decorations for capitals and mouldings—the patron had no say in this. The master mason also organised stone supplies. He subcontracted his team of masons, and was responsible for paying them. The lodge was the masons' headquarters on site. It was a workshop where masons could finish fine carving, and it was also used as a storage depot and even as a rest house.

The project at Durham would have required a large labour force of masons, stone cutters, hauliers, setters, quarrymen, smiths, carpenters, plumbers, glaziers, as well as minor workmen. Equipment would include carts, wagons, wheelbarrows, ropes and tackle. The master mason had to keep an expense account for the work.

The general workers consisted of a combination of artisans and unskilled labour. Under the mason were men with traditional craft skills and practices. Stone-dressing sheds would be built against previously completed walls. There was limited winter working, though much could be done under shelter, such as dressing and preparing stone. Carpenters played an essential role in all construction work, providing frameworks to support structures, as well as the timbers for the roofs. Smiths were required to maintain building tools. Carters ran teams of carthorses to pull loads of stone and timber to the site. They were responsible for the supply of fodder and horseshoes.

The semi-skilled workers applied numerical rules and simple geometry, and it was common knowledge that a right angle could be formed with a triangle of sides in the proportion 3:4:5. They were able to use a square and compasses, but most were illiterate and innumerate, and were not concerned with theorems or able to make calculations. Rods and cords were used to measure lengths.

Workers were concerned only with the stability of what they had built. So much relied on trial and error, and the collapse of part of the structure was accepted as the means to learn and improve the building process. Difficulties were overcome as they became apparent, and were accepted as a stimulus to creative ability.

William of St-Calais undertook to carry out the work on the church at his own expense,[9] and would have been "directly involved with the design of the building, not least for budgetary considerations, liturgical propriety, and the desire to ensure that his church was a worthy rival in scale and decoration to the grandest churches in Europe. He would therefore have formulated the brief in which the essential form of the building would have been determined".[10] But the bishop's greatest contribution was in his choice of the master mason responsible "for the translation of this brief into reality".[11]

Bilson considered the master mason to be a Norman who had been involved in work elsewhere in England before coming to Durham,[12] but Thurlby believed that he was of English, rather than Norman, origin, and suggested that he had probably been trained in the north of England. The parallels with Lastingham and York, noted above, led him to the opinion that "Perhaps it was at York that the Durham master honed his skills in vault construction before entering the employ of Bishop William".[13] Bony agreed with Thurlby—"The first Durham master . . . clearly was English, purely Saxon in sensibility, especially in his sense of plastic and linear values, but no less clearly Norman-trained and enjoying to the full the new Romanesqueness, more Norman even than any Norman in his use of exterior dado arcades".[14]

The skill of the master mason is evident to all who look at his work, but Bony's detailed study of the stonework of the first building campaign has revealed the extent of his genius. In the plinthwork alone we see the precision in the planning required for a building of this scale—Bony calculated that over 1500 blocks, cut to three set heights, had to be ordered from the quarries before work on the plinths could start.[15]

But it is the "mathematical elegance" with which he overcame the problem of the incised spiral pattern of the four piers in the choir that convinced Bony that the master mason "could outdo all continental builders in the handling of ashlar masonry. Producing there a virtuoso performance in rationalised stonework, he placed himself far ahead of all would-be competitors, technically at the apex of the most advanced modernity". "Nothing of the kind had been attempted before in medieval architecture: no previous example can be found of masonry work conceived and executed as the high precision assemblage of blocks cut in advance in such a way as to be not only interchangeable but reversible (a fine piece of template designing)".[16] "More remarkable still and more significant in terms of the mental training it pre-supposed is the amount of calculation and of advance designing carried to the minutest details of execution, which had had to be performed by the Durham master . . . to be able to order from the quarries those large series of perfectly shaped blocks that were so rapidly needed on the building site"[17] for the piers—a total of 920 blocks of one type, and 104 of another—"all impeccably sized and cut to templates", and a further 652 blocks in a semi-finished state, to be "carved in their finished form on the building site".[18]

The chronology of the building sequence established by Bilson in 1899, and developed by him in 1922,[19] is still considered "unshakeable".[20] He stated that "the design of the first master-mason was continued practically unaltered from the eastern arm into the transept, as far as the top of the triforium on the eastern side of both arms. The later parts of this first section of the work must, I think, have been built by the monks after the bishop's death, but it was not until the east side of the transept had been so far built that they introduced any serious modification of the first conception".[21] The lower parts of the presbytery triforium consist of dull-brown medium-grained sandstone, without visible mason's marks, while the work above is of fine-grained greyish-green stone with mason's marks. This distinction is also found in the east wall of the transepts and in the nave triforium above the eastern bays. It would seem that a new master mason obtained stone from a different quarry.

▲ *Building operations c.1180. Drawing by Rosemary Turner, based on a copy in Salzman* PLATE 5 *of a picture on folio 27v of the manuscript* Hortus Deliciarum, *written by the Abbess Herrard von Landsberg (1167–1195) at Hohenburg Abbey, Alsace (then in Germany). The original manuscript was destroyed by fire in 1870.*

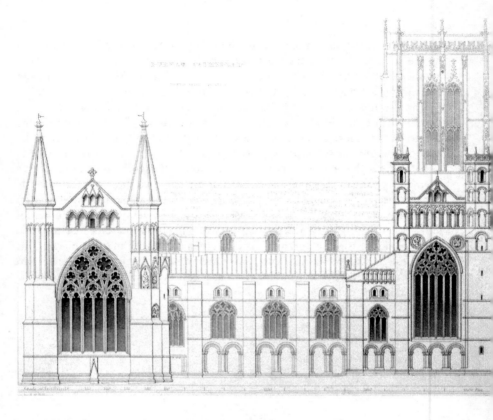

▲ *Durham Cathedral: north elevation, from Billings* PLATES VI-VII.

▼ *Durham Cathedral: longitudinal section of the north side, from Billings* PLATES X-XI.

Gallery over aisle

Clerestory

Major pier

Respond

Open arcade

Minor pier

Blind Arcade

Plinth

▲ *Durham Cathedral: section—the transepts looking east, from Billings* PLATE XIV.

Chronology of building work

1075x1080	Claustral buildings begun by Bishop Walcher.[22]
1088–91	Refectory completed during Bishop William's exile (undercroft survives).[23]
1092	Decision to build new cathedral.[24]
1093	First trench 29 July.[25] Foundation stone 11 August.[26] Outer walls of choir. Eastern apse foundations down 14 feet (4.25m) to rock.[27]
1094	Foundations of eastern walls of transepts. Choir piers and wall arcading begun.
1094–5	Choir piers and walls up to height of aisle vaults.
1096	Death of Bishop William of St-Calais. Monks continue building. Vault of choir aisles with rib-vaulting in east bays, completed by 1100.[28]
1098	All foundations laid including west front. Choir built up to window sills.
1099	Flambard made bishop. Work had been built "as far as the nave".[29]
1100	High vault of choir. Diagonal ribs made semi-circular so that the transverse arches were stilted to achieve same height. Quadripartite vault in double-bay units with transverse rib dividing the two bays.[30] Completed by 1104.
1101	Crossing arches and east walls of transepts.
1102–3	Semi-dome/vault of apse.
1102–3	Nave easternmost double bay and single bay built up to gallery.
1103–4	North transept up to triforium but not to vault. South transept wooden roof. Crossing surmounted by low belfry. Translation of St Cuthbert 29 August 1104.
1110–15	Vault of north transept (copied from choir).
1112	Chevrons over west door.
1113	Vault of crossing.
1115–18	Nave main arcades. Aisles roofed. Springing in nave with chevron decoration.
1116–25	South transept vaulted. Central clerestory pier cut to allow ribs. Structure supported from small tunnel vaults over passageway.[31]
1125–33	Walls of nave erected "up to its vault" [usque testudinem].[32]
1133	Nave completed.[33] West towers halted until gable built at west end.
1133–5	Choir-screen.[34]
1133–40	Chapter house completed—rib vault with keeled mouldings.[35]
c.1150	Dormitory completed during episcopate of William of St Barbara (1144–52).[36]

1170s	West end galilee built[37] (or even *c.*1165 because of chevron ornament).
*c.*1190	Shrine for Venerable Bede made in galilee.[38]
1195x1208	Prior's lodging under construction, perhaps on site of former dorter (now deanery).[39]
1235–40	Choir vault requires new build.[40]
1242	East end rebuilding begins.[41]
1244x1254	Chapel in prior's lodging built and, probably, undercroft of western dorter.[42]
1253	New high altar dedicated.[43]
1258x1290	Great tower built by prior Hugh of Darlington 1258–72, 1286–90.[44]
1270x1280	Choir revaulted.[45]
1290s	Vestry built south of presbytery.[46]
1366–74	New kitchen built by John Lewyn.[47]
1376–80	Neville screen built of Caen stone. New high altar dedicated 8 November 1380.[48]
1398–1404	Dorter in west range rebuilt.[49]
1406–19	Cloister remodelled—carrels installed.[50]
1414–15	Library begun above east parlour.[51] First purpose-built book room, 16 feet 6 inches (5m) by 60 feet (18m).
1419–30	Infirmary reconstructed.[52]
1429	Low Norman central tower destroyed by lightning 27 May 1429.[53]
1430–36	Prior's lodging and principal room of state in monastic guesthouse rebuilt.[54]
1432–33	New cloister laver constructed of Egglestone marble.[55]
1456	Tower again struck by lightning. Rebuilt 1464–89.[56]

The presbytery

The presbytery was basically an aisled hall with an eastern apse, flanked by two smaller apses encased in square walls which may have supported towers. In order to enhance this important part of the church, the master mason constructed piers which encircled the intended site of the shrine of St Cuthbert. To provide a suitable canopy over the shrine, he embarked on the use of stone vaulting. The apse was rib-vaulted to complete the three-part division given by the wall-shafts. This also involved the crossing piers and the columnar piers in the transepts. All were conceived as part of the overall design, creating a harmonious whole. The western bays of the presbytery are reduced in width because they were set out to agree with the width of the transept aisles.

The presbytery consists of two double-bays which meet a solid wall of the subsidiary apses. The aisles have blank arcading with interlacing arches of multiform moulding. The aisle vaulting was effected with cross-ribs with refined mouldings. The transverse arches rest on tripartite shafts against the outer walls. The central piers alternate between compound and circular with spiral grooving. The alternate massive cylindrical pillars stop short of the clerestory but they are interspersed with piers bearing clustered columns that ascend all the way to the stone vault. The quadripartite vaulting was designed for two oblong vaults over each double-bay, with a transverse arch at both the major and minor piers.[57] A wooden screen behind the high altar gave access to the shrine.

▼ *Durham Cathedral: the choir in 1841—looking west, from Billings* PLATE LI.

Durham Cathedral: mouldings in the choir

Base-moulding: the bases of the Durham choir pillars were moulded with double hollow-chamfer *c.*1095.

The plinth-moulding has a raised projecting course, chamfered top and bottom, and uses a pre-Conquest motif.

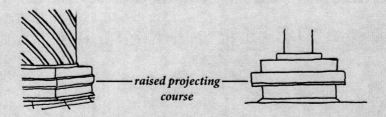

raised projecting course

▲ *Plinth of piers in crossing, transept and nave (not to scale)*

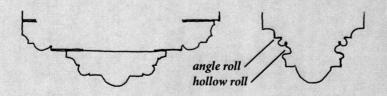

angle roll
hollow roll

▲ *Arch-moulding: arcade c.1095*

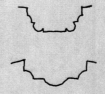

▶ *Vaulting-ribs:*
cross-arch (above),
rib (below) c.1095

▼ *Piers: major (left), minor (centre), arcade arch (right)*

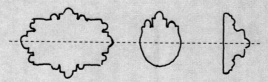

Illustrations by Rosemary Turner, based on drawings
by Billings, Bilson and the author.

The eastern apse

An apse was introduced to a building to terminate a vista and to give an architectural setting for a special object or shrine. The concavity was its significant element. The Durham apse contained a high vault, probably roofed at a lower level than the choir.

The easternmost triforium arches of the presbytery have shafted jambs which point north and south. This suggests that a major transverse arch was at the entrance to the sanctuary, supporting the eastern gable. The sanctuary and apse were probably treated as a separate architectural feature attached to the east-end gable of the presbytery.

The interlaced arcading appeared on the walls of all the apses, the aisles and the sanctuary bay.[58] The latter probably had a ribbed quadripartite vault similar to that originally in the choir.[59] The three apses were each covered with a ribbed stone vault in the semi-domes. There must have been a positive decision not to create a crypt below the shrine.

By 1235 cracks and fissures had appeared in the apse semi-dome and the forebay,[60] due to the experimental character of the vaulting. This "may have resulted from the settlement of the Romanesque towers above the aisle apses which flanked the forebay".[61] The apses were therefore demolished and the Chapel of the Nine Altars built between 1242 and 1275. At the same time the entire choir vault was replaced to blend with the new work.[62]

The foundations of the former apses were uncovered in 1895.[63] Some of the masonry in the inner face of the aisle apse foundations is constructed of unusual-sized stones. They are longer in proportion to their height, which is not the style used by the Normans. They have been worked with pre-Conquest tooling, and not axed diagonally. These dressed stones must be re-used material from Aldhun's church of 996–9.[64]

Interlaced arcading

There appears to have been a desire to continue the Anglo-Saxon tradition of decorating flat surfaces. The exterior decoration at ground level at Durham consists of round-headed arcading, previously unknown in England. The apse of the church of St-Étienne, Caen, built in 1067 with some arcading, may have been a prototype. The arcading at Durham is much more expressive, in that it has two orders, which would have required extra centring for each arch.

Inside, along the aisle walls of the presbytery, is further linear decoration where interlaced arcading forms a dado. The design seems to have been derived from Islamic ideas.

The exterior dado of the transepts of Christchurch Priory also has interlacing arches, which might suggest that Flambard copied the idea from Durham. Work there began c.1093, ceased in 1099 when Flambard was otherwise engaged, and resumed between 1110 and 1115.

▲ *Durham Cathedral: interlaced arcading at the west end of the nave, from Billings* PLATE XXXVIII.

The transepts

The transepts only have aisles on the eastern side, providing space for chapels. The major piers here are of the same depth as those in the choir, but their breadth has been reduced to provide adequate width for the chapel entrances.[65] As in the choir, there is a gallery over each aisle, but the clerestory wall passages in the transepts contrast with the solid-walled clerestory in the choir.[66] The western side of the north transept has a 25-inch wide (0.64m) triforium passage in place of the gallery, accessed from the stair turret in the north-west angle of the transept, necessitating the use of corbels to support the vault.[67]

Financial restraints may have led to a temporary abandonment of the plan for a stone vault in the south transept, as Bilson believed that "the simple tall continuous [clerestory] arcade is obviously designed for a ceiling of wood". The stone vault was ultimately installed, perhaps as a result of increased offerings after the translation of 1104, which also enabled the north transept to be vaulted, with miniature shafted arcadings in a form later adopted in the nave clerestory. The north transept high vault of c.1110 is probably the earliest surviving example with diagonal ribs. The north transept clerestory arcade fits the lunette of the vault. The wall passage is about 7 feet 6 inches (2.3m) high, whilst that in the south is almost 12 feet (3.6m).[68]

The crossing

The transepts at Durham are wider than the nave, so the crossing is not square. In order to have the same sized openings on all four sides, the east–west responds are longer than the south–north responds. The piers of the crossing are deliberately designed asymmetrically and the east–west respond is even decorated with a half-shaft to pick up the flow of the shaft on the soffit faces of the east and west jambs.

The crossing is 40 feet (12.2m) across from the centres of the great columns. The crossing arches were part of the first building campaign, and were constructed by about 1100. In each of the four angles is a single attached shaft, but the vaulting may not have been completed.

The tower was not completed until 1490, to a height of 216 feet (66m). It contains a staircase in the south-west corner.

The nave

The main arcades of the nave were erected between 1104 and 1109, and consisted of three double-bays with a single western bay. The bays are divided by engaged shafts running up to the vaulted roof. No doubt the building of the nave walls and arcades up to the vaulting can be attributed to Flambard. Work continued intermittently until his death in 1128, depending on the availability of finance.[69]

Durham's nave shows alternation of piers and columns with designs of chevrons, lozenges, flutings and spirals. The alternation of clustered columns and single columns was copied from Jumièges. The chevron pattern is taken up in the mouldings of the triforium arches, the clerestory windows, and the vaulting ribs themselves, with additional fret carvings. The pier ornamentation was originally painted red and black.[70] There are even two cylindrical piers at the west end which have twenty-four vertical flutes, following the advice of Vitruvius when describing Ionic architecture.[71] Many monastic libraries possessed copies of his treatise, written

▼ *Durham Cathedral: the nave in 1841 looking east, from Billings* PLATE XLI.

about AD 18, so there was an awareness of his precepts. An eighth-century copy of Vitruvius compiled at Jarrow is now in the British Library.[72]

Some arches are richly ornamented with the chevron design, which was not introduced until well after 1100. "The innovation was to have a more immediate and widespread significance for the development of Anglo-Norman Romanesque than the more spectacular and more famous introduction of 'rib-vaults'."[73] The earliest chevron decoration is in the dormitory at Canterbury (1080s), but not in any quantity. The slype doorway jambs at Durham may show some chevron decoration.

Chevrons appear on the main arcade in the third bay westward from the crossing, the second bay of the gallery and the first bay of the clerestory.

The arcades in the nave are of a similar height to those in the presbytery, as the floor level is the same and there is no crypt beneath the presbytery.

The nave was planned to have a wooden roof but so many years elapsed while building the walls that the scheme was abandoned and the plans changed, in order to accommodate a high vault.[74] The nave walls were built up to the gallery before the decision was made to vault. This is apparent from the facts that corbels had to be provided, suggesting a change of intention, and that the clerestory windows are centred on the later vault and not on the gallery bays already built. The centre of these windows is more towards the centre of the double bays than the gallery arches. The diagonal aisle ribs of the nave had simple hollows but gave way to the torus roll. This appears on the second order of the transverse arches and the main arcade arches.

The nave vault was built in connection with the clerestory.[75] In the absence of sill-set shafts to carry the diagonal ribs of the high vault, the ribs had to be set on corbels of the same type as used in the west wall of the south transept. Opportunity was taken to avoid the flattening of the crown arch with a Romanesque semi-circle design, and to introduce pointed transverse arches. It has been suggested that the quadrant arches of the galleries provide abutment for the high vault and are forerunners of flying buttresses. However, being originally less than 15 inches (38cm) thick, they "were not conceived as buttresses for the high vault but rather as supports for a novel roof system with transverse gables".[76]

The clerestory has one sizeable window per bay, with nook-shafts and a moulded arch. The windows have a zigzag decoration. A corbel-table completes the elevation. The clerestory, with its tall arch in the centre and a small arch at each side, is similar to that at Waltham, though the triforia are not alike.

The triforium of Durham has the same design as that at Christchurch Priory, and both were built by Ranulf Flambard. "One bold semi-circular arch, with double columns separated by square members, encloses a subordinate arrangement of coupled arches supported on a single column".[77] The triforium openings consist of two sub-arches under one containing arch with a blind tympanum.

The construction of the nave vault was begun after Flambard's death in 1128 and was not completed until 1133.[78] It used the rib in conjunction with the pointed arch. The webbing of the vaults became progressively thinner as work proceeded westerly. It varies from 15¾ inches (40cm) at the east end to 12 inches (30cm) at the west end. The nave vault is 10 feet 2 inches (3.1m) behind the clerestory arches level, but only 8 feet 5 inches (2.57m) behind the springers of the high vault.

The first hint of the pointed arch can be seen in the main arches of the nave, which rise from the piers and divide the vaulting of the bays.[79] The vault shafts terminate at the base of the triforium. The triforium consists of a wall-passage fronted by an open arcade, as at Gloucester. The vault shafts emphasise horizontal layers as opposed to the vertical emphasis of the French Gothic. The double bays in the nave create two oblong spaces between the main piers. The diagonal ribs in each bay

▲ *Triforium of the choir—south side, from Billings* PLATE LIII.

▼ *Triforium of the nave—north side, from Billings* PLATE XLIII.

are semicircular, resulting in the transverse arch becoming a pointed arch. The idea derives from Cluny III (dedicated 1128), also built with a hint of the future. This was destined to revolutionise vaulting construction in western Europe. The transverse arches are struck from centres below the springing line. There are no transverse ribs on the minor piers, but diagonal ribs on corbels.

When Geoffrey Rufus became bishop in 1133 the cathedral had been finished, enabling him to concentrate on completing the chapter house,[80] where he was buried in 1141. Other developments followed over the centuries, especially the replacement of the original eastern apse with the Chapel of the Nine Altars, and the building of the galilee at the west end, but Turgot's cathedral, "one of the great experiences of Europe",[81] still stands as witness to the achievement of the prior and his associates.

The claustral buildings

According to Symeon, Bishop Walcher intended to establish a monastery at Durham. "For which reason he laid the foundations and began to construct buildings for monks at Durham, on the site which they now occupy".[82] Excavations in 1903 uncovered the original west wall of the cloister, 2 feet 6 inches (1.75m) wide and traced from north to south for 54 feet 6 inches (16.6m).[83] The evidence suggests that this earliest cloister was 115 feet (35m) square,[84] but it was later extended to the north and west after the demolition of the Saxon cathedral. Perhaps this is the meaning of the statement by the continuator of Symeon that Flambard "extended the cramped precinct of the monks by a considerable distance widthways and lengthways".[85] However, surviving stonework from the laver built in the south-west corner of the original cloister garth has been dated to the late twelfth century (see p. 80). It has been assumed that this first cloister was laid out to fit the Saxon cathedral,[86] but work in the 1980s, using dowsing, suggests that the Saxon building was sited within the cloister garth (see plan on p. 58), with the sanctuary centred on the wall between the chapter house and the slype *cum* parlour.[87] This was the position of St Cuthbert's cenotaph according to sixteenth-century descriptions, some of which state that his coffin had remained here in 'the White Church' until 1104.[88]

If the earliest cloister was not set out in relation to the Saxon cathedral, it follows that there were already plans at this stage to replace the old building. Walcher began on the east side of the proposed cloister, but it is unlikely that work had progressed beyond the ground floor before he died in 1080. The earliest complete building is that used as a strongroom or prison, consisting of three rooms. Nearest to the chapter house was the chapel, measuring 23 by 12 feet (7 by 3.7m). A fresco on the south wall depicted Christ as judge. A triangular-headed recess at the north end of the west wall of this room is of Saxon style. The second room was for the warder's use and contained a hatch to provide meagre rations. The adjoining cell was 8 feet (2.4m) square with a low ceiling, only 6 feet 6 inches (2m) high in the centre. There was a latrine in the thickness of the wall.[89] This prison was only used for short-term sentences.

It was not until William of St-Calais was in exile (1088–91) that Turgot finished building the dining hall in the south range of the cloister.[90] The undercroft survives

◀ *Durham Cathedral: the*
prison in which the monks were
confined for short sentences.
Watercolour by Rosemary
Turner based on a 1929
drawing by Gordon Home. [91]

but the upper storey was rebuilt in the seventeenth century.[92] The undercroft has rude groined vaults supported on 3 feet 3 inch (1m) piers. A dais at the east end was two steps above the main floor and ran across the whole width of the frater, to a depth of 13 feet (4m).[93]

The earliest dorter or dormitory was in the south-east corner of the cloister. The undercroft, a two-aisled Norman construction with a tunnel-vault, now supports the deanery, formerly the prior's lodging. The walls of the early-Norman reredorter are visible in the great hall of the deanery.[94] However, when the chapter house was erected to its full height it prevented access from the dormitory to the south transept.[95] This was probably one reason why the dormitory was transferred to the western range of the cloister, conveniently bringing the new reredorter closer to the river. The present western undercroft dates from the early thirteenth century, but the doorway at the north end is part of a twelfth-century predecessor.[96] It has been suggested that the lower parts of the east wall of the existing western range incorporate part of the *west* wall of the earlier range.[97] Bishop William of St Barbara (1144–52) is said to have completed the dormitory, though its location is not stated.[98]

Bishops Walcher, William of St-Calais and Ranulf Flambard were all buried in the chapter house, but the existing walls date from soon after St-Calais's death, and it was not completed until the time of Flambard's successor, Geoffrey Rufus (1133–41).[99] It is in the middle of the east side not of the present cloister, but of the earlier, smaller, cloister.[100] The vaulting ribs have a soffit roll flanked by a row of sunk star ornaments with chevrons, later than the nave vault, so after 1133.[101] The chapter house has arcades of interlacing arches with a zigzag frieze above and shows refinement of the mouldings with early use of 'keeling' (shafts supporting interlacing round arches). The eastern portion was demolished in 1796, but rebuilt in 1895.

Between the chapter house and the south transept was the slype, a passageway to the cemetery which doubled as a 'parlour' or place of conversation.[102] It is coeval with the chapter house and also has arcades of interlacing arches with a zigzag frieze above, but has a tunnel-vaulted roof. In 1414/15 a library was built above it.[103]

▼ *Durham Cathedral: east walk of the cloister, from Billings* PLATE XLIV.

The laver

Before entering the dining hall (*frater*) for meals, the monks washed their hands in the cloister. Often a long trough was used, with water running in at one end and out at the other. Sometimes a long pipe delivered jets of water through a series of spouts.

It was the responsibility of the fraterer to look after the laver. At Barnwell, Cambridge, he ensured that it was always clean and working properly, and the fraterer was also to provide sand and a whetstone for sharpening knives.[104]

The twelfth-century laver at Durham was excavated in March/April 1903 by W. H. St. John Hope.[105] It was situated in the south-west corner of the original cloister garth, within an area 15 feet (4.6m) square, and its north and east sides had foundations 2 feet (0.6m) in width. The south and west sides used the arcade walling of the cloister garth.

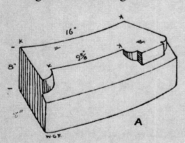

The laver consisted of two circles of stonework. The inner was about 4 feet (1.2m) in diameter, and the outer had an internal diameter of 6 feet (1.8m) and an external diameter of about 7 feet 6 inches (2.3m). The actual laver with basins was supported on an outer low circular wall of ashlar stone. The space between the inner and outer circles was left hollow to allow access to the pipes.

Illustration A shows a stone worked in the same curve as the foundation with a broad chamfer. The chamfer has footings for a series of vertical ribs (illustration B) 6½ inches (16cm) wide, and 9⅝ inches (24cm) apart, which if continued round would divide the outer face of the wall into fifteen compartments. Pieces of worked stone nearby indicate that the laver was enclosed by an open arcade.

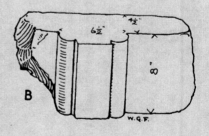

Illustration C shows a voussoir with a bold zigzag moulding on each face, and D one with a roll on each side. The decoration suggests a late twelfth-century date.

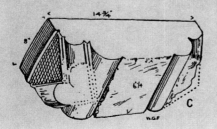

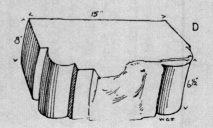

Water was originally obtained from a well in the cloister. This was also excavated in 1903 and found to be lined with ashlar stone and surmounted by a plain coping. It has an internal diameter of 4 feet (1.2m), the lower part sunk into rock to a total depth of some 47 feet (14.3m). Beside the well would have been a large standpipe under a cistern, which was filled manually from the well. A stone channel, about 9 inches (23cm) wide, runs from the site of this standpipe to the laver, and contained lead piping with an external diameter of 2¾ inches (7cm). The gradient between standpipe and laver is 1:15. Another stone channel, 6 inches (15cm) wide, led in a south-westerly direction, towards the kitchen area. Early in the thirteenth century the system for providing water was changed and the laver was supplied from a conduit situated on the highest point of the precinct, south of the monastic kitchen.[106] The main conduit was supplied with water from springs on the west side of the river Wear, and brought by pipes to the precinct. Water was then distributed by gravitation through lead pipes to lavers, kitchen, bakehouse, brewhouse, etc. On the occasions when the pipes were blocked or frozen, it was necessary to revert to the manual system in the cloister. The Bursar's Roll for 1338/9 refers to "drawing water from the draw-well in the cloister" because the pipe to various offices was frozen.[107]

The laver was rebuilt in the early thirteenth century, after the cloister had been enlarged. The new octagonal structure extended over the western wall of the old cloister. In 1432–3 it was provided with new marble basins fitted with twenty-four brass taps.[108] A detailed description survives from the sixteenth century.[109] The basin and trough now stand in the centre of the cloister garth.

▲ *Durham Cathedral: the laver basin and trough in the cloister garth in 1841. Detail from Billings* PLATE XLV *(see* FRONTISPIECE*).*

▲ *Durham Cathedral: the west end of the chapter house in 1795.*
Sketch by John Carter from Greenwell, Drawings PLATE III.

CHAPTER 6

Turgot the Writer

Since the seventeenth century Turgot has often been credited as the author of many works, including the *Libellus de exordio atque procursu istius, hoc est Dunhelmensis, ecclesie* (*Tract on the Origins and Progress of this the Church of Durham*) and *Historia regum Anglorum* (*History of the Kings of England*), the main sources of information for this study.[1] Late twelfth-century manuscripts of the *Historia regum*[2] and the *Libellus de exordio*[3] have rubrics attributing them to one of Turgot's fellow monks, Symeon of Durham, but the earliest manuscripts of the latter, both dating from the earliest twelfth century, are anonymous, though one is annotated in Symeon's own hand.[4] However, Turgot's authorship of these was thoroughly refuted by Thomas Rud in 1732, and modern scholars have found further evidence from palaeography that they were, in fact, compiled by Symeon, albeit at Turgot's command.[5]

Symeon's handwriting shows that he was from northern France or Normandy, and he was probably one of three scribes who came to Durham with William of St-Calais on the bishop's return from exile in 1091, joining the monastic community there as its thirty-eighth member.[6] By 1096 he was a senior monk, and in 1104 he witnessed the miracle of the incorruptible body of St Cuthbert at the translation, when he "held a candlestick with its waxlight, continually amid his flowing tears impressed sweet kisses upon those sacred feet".[7] He was cantor or precentor by 1126, and probably died about 1128. Symeon's day in the Kalendar was 14 October.

Symeon was a compiler of records, rather than an author, as he himself admits in his preface to the *Libellus de exordio*: "I have gathered together and set out in order those things which I have been able to find scattered through the documents".[8] In assembling his *Historia regum*, Symeon added little of his own material, simply reproducing earlier histories, such as a compilation by Byrhtferth of Ramsey (*c.*970–*c.*1020), itself drawn from other writers, extracts from William of Malmesbury's *De gestis regum*, and a chronicle derived from John of Worcester for 848–1118.[9] This was a time without copyright restrictions. He used a similar approach in compiling the *Libellus de exordio*. Palaeographical research has identified his handwriting in copies of Bede's *Vita S. Cuthberti* and *Historia ecclesiastica*, and the *Historia de Sancto Cuthberto*. As Rollason points out, "All these texts were heavily used as sources for the *Libellus de exordio*, and it is almost as if we are seeing Symeon collecting materials for that work".[10]

It is likely that Symeon obtained much of his more recent information from Turgot, and it is quite possible that Turgot had already committed some of this material to writing, and that Symeon used this as another of his sources. There are certainly similarities between Symeon's description of Bishop William of St-Calais—"his sternness was not rigid nor his gentleness lax, so that he tempered one with the other, making his severity jocund and his jocundity severe"[11]—and Turgot's description of Queen Margaret who "possessed so great pleasantness with severity, that all who were in her service, men and women, both loved her with fear, and feared her with love: ... For she repressed in herself every vice, and was very serious in rejoicing, very upright in anger",[12] or the introductory address of the

Life of St Margaret—"Requesting, you have commanded, and in commanding have requested".[13]

However, the accusation of plagiarism made by Selden in the mid-seventeenth century,[14] and repeated by William Hutchinson in the late eighteenth century,[15] cannot be upheld. In quoting Symeon, Hutchinson refers to "Turgot (alias Symeon)".[16] The persistence of these erroneous attributions is an interesting indication of Turgot's reputation as a writer of significant works.

As well as attributing what he considered to be the original draft of the *Libellus de exordio* to Turgot,[17] Hutchinson also stated that "He wrote the Life of King Malcolm and his queen Margaret, of the kings of the Scots, Annals of his Own Times, and Chronicle of Durham".[18]

If this statement is correct, the only work of Turgot to survive is the *Life of St Margaret Queen of Scotland*.[19] In the earliest extant manuscript, now in the British Library, the author of this work merely calls himself "T., servant of the servants of St Cuthbert", but in a later manuscript, now in Madrid, he is identified as Turgot.[20] He was certainly recognised as its author by John of Tynemouth, a St Albans monk who included a précis of this work in a collection of English saints' lives in the

◀ *Monastic scribe of the mid-12th century. Drawing by Rosemary Turner, based on Cambridge, Trinity College MS R.17.1 fol. 283v.*

second quarter of the fourteenth century, in which he stated "at length, having called her confessor, Turgot, second prior of Durham, she began to relate her life".[21] John of Fordun, the Scottish chronicler who died c.1384, similarly believed that it was written by Turgot, though he also mistakenly attributed to Turgot some statements from the writings of Aelred of Rievaulx (died 1167),[22] which has given support to the idea that some of Turgot's historical writings have been lost.

Other suggestions have been made as to the author of the *Life of St Margaret*. One manuscript expands the "T." into "Theodericus".[23] A monk named "Theodricus" is number 130 in Symeon's list, too low in the list to be the author. Another candidate is Thurstin, number 76 on the list, on the grounds that "the Prior of Durham could not have been so frequent a visitor as the author of the *Vita* evidently was", and that the author was apparently sacristan of the church at Dunfermline.[24] However, Turgot's responsibilities as acting archdeacon of the diocese of Durham, which extended into Lothian, would have required frequent visits into southern Scotland, and the author does not state that he was sacristan at Dunfermline, but merely that he had care of the vessels of that church for some time. The description of the author as "servant of the servants of St Cuthbert" seems more appropriate for a prior than for an ordinary monk, and there is no valid reason for doubting Turgot's authorship.

When Margaret's daughter, Edith, became Queen Matilda of England in 1100, she wished to learn more of her mother's life, and naturally turned to Turgot, who had been closely associated with her (see next chapter). The *Life of St Margaret* was written at Durham between 1100 and 1107, during the reign of Margaret's son, Edgar (1097–1107).[25] The work is not a biography of the saint, but more a character sketch of the queen, detailing her achievements. It has been described as "a 'mirror' or didactic tool for the new queen of England, presenting the virtues of an ideal or perfect princess".[26] A translation is reproduced in the Appendix.

Malcolm and Margaret both died in 1093, and it is not inconceivable that Turgot had begun to write their biographies at that time. The period from 1091 to 1096 was probably the least busy part of his priorate, and he had access to a large monastic library enhanced by the gifts of Bishop William of St-Calais. When the bishop died in 1096 Turgot became fully occupied in running the affairs of the large bishopric as archdeacon, as well as ensuring that cathedral building continued until the eastern part was completed in 1104.

As prior, Turgot encouraged the monks to add to the library, not only by copying and illuminating manuscripts, but also by creating new works. The monastery at Durham produced many gifted writers during the twelfth century—Turgot himself and Symeon, as well as the authors of *De miraculis*, and later Lawrence (d.1154), Reginald (fl.1162–1173) and Germanus (d.1189).[27] This was appropriate in a community that looked to St Cuthbert for its origins, and to Bede for its inspiration. The monks of old Celtic monasteries, amidst the Norman newcomers, recalled the past "to give the community its identity in the present".[28]

Durham Cathedral: south-east view from Elvet Banks, from Billings PLATE XXVII.

CHAPTER 7

Turgot, Friend of Scotland

Turgot's appointment as bishop of St Andrews was not his first contact with Scotland. He had spent a short time at Melrose with the monk Aldwin around 1080, but the threatening demands of the Scottish king, Malcolm III Canmore (1058–1093), soon brought about their recall by Bishop Walcher (see chapter 2).

There were no strict diocesan boundaries at this time, but it was acknowledged that tenants living along the east coast between the Firth of Forth and the Tay were to be under the bishop of St Andrews, while those in Lothian, south of the Forth, were subject to Durham.

King Malcolm was an uncultured warrior who raided English settlements at every opportunity. In 1070 he attacked several churches in Northumbria including Wearmouth. The churches may have been deemed fortified positions, and Malcolm wished to show his prowess as a war leader. It was said that at this time no household in Scotland lacked an English slave-girl.[1] Later that year he married, as his second wife, Margaret, a descendant of the Saxon royal house. Margaret ransomed many captives, particularly the English.[2] She must have been relieved that, when William the Norman came by sea to Scotland in 1072, Malcolm swore homage to the 'English' king, promising not to harbour refugees from England,[3] though Malcolm did not cease his depredations across the border.

Turgot and the queen

A strong relationship was built up between the queen and Prior Turgot in the years 1086–7, when the bishop of Durham was away, attending to King William I and affairs of state, and again in 1088–91 when the bishop was living in exile in Normandy. Their friendship may have begun when he was appointed prior in 1087, and the queen was founding a monastery at Dunfermline Palace. She asked him to take charge of the sacred vessels of the church that the king and queen had built at the palace, and Turgot did so for "a long time".[4] The royal church at Dunfermline was dedicated to the Holy Trinity, with a threefold desire for the salvation of the king, the queen, and their children. Turgot was to have an important part to play in the education of the royal children. In connection with her new monastic foundation at the palace, the queen would wish to learn more about monasticism, and the prior could expound on the discipline of community life and the tradition of praying, listening and learning. The resultant stimulation of enquiry would always be present.

Turgot was not without experience in conversing with royalty. He had worked with King Olav (1066–93) in Norway for many years, and in 1091, when the bishop of Durham was in exile, he had had dealings with William Rufus of England. The queen would want to know about the Norwegian court, and his experiences in that country. Turgot maintained close contact with the kings of Scotland—Malcolm and his sons Duncan, Edgar and Alexander.

St Margaret of Scotland

Margaret was the grand-daughter of King Edmund Ironside (1016), and grand-niece of Edward the Confessor (1043–66). When Edmund's father, King Æthelred II, died in April 1016, Cnut of Denmark, who had invaded England, displaced Edmund, who died under mysterious circumstances in November 1016. According to Symeon and other chroniclers, Cnut sent Edmund's infant sons, Edmund and Edward, to be slaughtered by the Swedish king, who instead sent them to Hungary. However, their journey to Hungary seems to have taken place some years later. Adam of Bremen (c.1080) and the anonymous scribe who compiled *Leges Edwardi Confessoris Regis* c.1130 under Margaret's son-in-law, King Henry I of England, both record that the boys went to Russia—the wife of Grand Duke Jaroslav I of Kiev (1019–54) may have been the boys' aunt.[5] There they met and befriended the exiled sons of Basil (Vazul), cousin and heir to King Stephen of Hungary, and there too Edward met, and around 1043 married, Agatha, daughter of the brother (*germanus*) of Holy Roman Emperor Henry III (1039–56), probably his half-brother, Liudulf of West Friesland.[6] Following Stephen's death in 1038, a year after Basil had been killed, civil war broke out in Hungary, and in 1046 Basil's eldest son, Andrew, who had married a daughter of Jaroslav, returned to Hungary to claim his crown, accompanied by Edward and Agatha. (A dark cloud surrounds the fate of Edward's brother, Edmund, who appears to have made a royal princess pregnant and disappears from the records.[7])

Agatha proved a worthy consort of Edward. She was resolute and of great help in the turbulent times. They had their own property in Hungary. Margaret was born in 1046 and was given her name, probably, from the cult of St Margaret of Antioch. The name *Margarita* or *Margarite* is Old French for pearl, which later reminded Turgot, the author of her *Life*, that Margaret was a pearl of great price.[8] Christina was born about 1049, followed in about 1052 by Edgar. The children were brought up with a strong catholic faith.

In 1054 King Edward (later called the Confessor)[9] heard of the presence in Hungary of Edward the Exile (*d'Outremer*), and sent an embassy, headed by Bishop Ealdred of Worcester, to bring the family back to England. As his sole next of kin, Prince Edward would be declared heir to the English throne. Although they received a warm welcome from the people, who rejoiced that a son of Edmund Ironside had returned, the reaction of Edward the Exile's family must have been one of bemusement. True, this was their homeland, but they were not able to speak English, and even found themselves dressed differently.

However, Edward never met his uncle, the king, but died within a few days of arrival, on 19 April 1057, from an unknown cause, probably poison. His family was supported by the king until he died on 6 January 1066, Margaret and Christina receiving their education at the royal court. They were taught to read sacred manuscripts in Latin and were introduced to the lives of saints, the teachings of Gregory and Cassian, and the works of Augustine.

The king of Scotland, Malcolm, had also been brought up in King Edward's court until 1054. On 25 April 1058 he was inaugurated as king in a ceremony outside the church at Scone in Scotland. Soon after, he married Ingibjorg, widow of the earl of Orkney, Thorfinn Sigurdson. In 1059 Malcolm visited King Edward at Gloucester. There he would have met Margaret, aged 13, though he was unlikely to have paid much attention to her at this meeting.

When William the Norman invaded England, Margaret was of age but her only brother, Edgar the Ætheling (meaning throne-worthy), was only 14. As a possible claimant to the throne of England, Edgar had to submit to William at Berkhamsted in December 1066. In the spring of 1067 William took Edgar and other English nobles with him to Normandy, not returning until December. Margaret and Christina remained in England with their mother.

A rebellion in northern England began at Whitsuntide 1068 and Edgar and family took a boat to Scotland where King Malcolm gave them refuge.[10] The historian Symeon of Durham refers to the prince being received with his sisters, "beautiful girls of the royal blood".[11] Aelred of Rievaulx (1110–67) says that the emperor had sent the family to England "with great honour and wealth",[12] but John of Fordun (d.c.1384), who mistakenly ascribes to Turgot several passages from Aelred,[13] attributes their wealth to King Edward, saying that Margaret "had abundant riches, which her uncle, the king of England, had formerly given to her father . . . and a very large share thereof the holy queen brought over with her to Scotland. She brought, besides, many relics of saints, more precious than any stone or gold. Among these was that holy Cross, which they call the *black*, no less feared than loved by all Scottish men, through veneration for its holiness".[14] (This description of the relic is taken from Aelred, not Turgot.[15]) The Black Cross or 'Holy Rood' was an ebony casket shaped as a cross and decorated with gold, silver and ivory, that was believed to contain a portion of the cross of Christ.

In February 1069 Queen Ingibjorg of Scotland died, and Malcolm decided to make Margaret his new queen, and she reluctantly agreed. She would not be daunted by this new environment—many queen-consorts had to learn a new language and customs. The kings of Scotland usually held court at Dunkeld or Abernethy, on the Tay, but Malcolm chose the castle at Dunfermline near the river Forth.

The marriage took place in the palace chapel of Dunfermline in the spring of 1069, solemnised by Bishop Fothad II mac Maolmhicheil of St Andrews.[16] Margaret soon turned Malcolm's scantily furnished fort into a royal abode, where they entertained in style. The existing church would have consisted of a simple oblong cell, but around 1072 Malcolm and Margaret founded the new church of the Holy Trinity, Dunfermline, which became part of the palace. Margaret decorated it sumptuously, providing a large cross bearing the image of the Saviour, plated with gold and silver and encrusted with jewels.[17]

In 1074 Malcolm claimed sovereignty over the Western Isles, which had been under Norwegian rule but had succumbed to an Irish chief, Diarmed, who died in 1072. Danish raiders from Limerick had attacked the islands in 973, and in 986 they had killed all at Iona. In 1070 the abbot of Iona had been killed by another Irish chief. Queen Margaret would have been overjoyed that she could make contact with Iona and the followers of St Columba. She wished to restore Iona and attend to the decay of its clergy. She "rebuilt it, and furnished it with monks, with an endowment for performing the Lord's work".[18]

Queen Margaret had found nothing in Scotland resembling the monastic life familiar in the western church, following the Rule of St Benedict. She wished to introduce non-Celtic monasticism into Scotland. At Dunfermline were numerous chaplains (*capellani*) and the king and queen wished for it to become a monastery, as a daughter house of Canterbury, so they requested assistance from Archbishop Lanfranc (1070–89), who sent them three monks.[19] The abbey church and monastic buildings were not completed in the lifetimes of Malcolm and Margaret, and their son, King Edgar (1097–1107), asked for more monks, who were supplied by Anselm, archbishop of Canterbury.[20]

Margaret exceeded the requirements of the church in fasting. Pope Gregory VII (1073–85) curtailed the fast of Advent to the four Sundays, but she began midweek on 15 November, before Advent Sunday. Her extreme abstinence may have contributed towards her final illness—"by excessive abstinence she brought on the molestation of a very serious disease".[21]

Archbishop Lanfranc (1070–1089) was Margaret's confessor and had been flattered when asked. He expressed surprise that a queen "born of a royal line, brought up as befits a queen . . . should choose me a man of foreign birth, without worth, as your father . . . Henceforth therefore may I be your father and, as for you, be my daughter".[22]

After Lanfranc's death in 1089, Turgot may have been invited to become her confessor. If not as confessor, he certainly became the queen's confidential friend and spiritual adviser. As superior of the monastery he was permitted to administer the sacraments, which included the hearing of confessions. He was probably made a priest when appointed prior; as archdeacon, he could not have exercised his responsibility for parish clergy unless he were a priest.

The queen was deeply religious, having acquired her cultural and spiritual values at the court of St Stephen in Hungary when very young, and later at the court of Edward the Confessor. She impressed the royal court in Scotland with her culture and her Christian principles, and led the nation along new paths of worship in religion. She wished to bring practices in the Scottish church into line with those with which she was familiar, and worked for the due observance of Sundays, festivals, fasts, annual communion and marriage customs, and the cessation of simony, usury and 'incestuous' marriages. However, she was sympathetic to Scottish churchmen and, following earlier Scottish kings, gave endowments to the Iona community and others. Margaret arranged a conference around 1090 to discuss all these matters. In the absence of the bishop, she would have sought guidance from Turgot in her preparations. The meeting went on for three days, supported by the king, who proved an essential link between the Scots, who spoke no English, and the queen, who spoke little Gaelic (though she spoke many languages and was at home in any environment).

Margaret entered fully into the Scottish ways, but also introduced new fashions—and standards of acceptability—in dress, as she found Scotland lacking in these aspects of life, compared to the rest of Europe. In the palace she set up a "workshop of celestial art" for the ladies of the court, to make and embroider altar linen and vestments.[23] Secular and ecclesiastical architecture became more elaborate and dignified. The palace glittered with gold and silver.[24] She maintained courtliness, always performing what the royal dignity required. However, her private life was most austere; she ate sparingly and permitted herself little sleep. She issued regulations to curb unnecessary expenditure and discouraged unrestrained laughter.[25] She followed a monastic routine and rose at midnight and went to her chapel for matins, the king often sharing her vigil.

Malcolm was rough and uncultured but with a kind disposition. Margaret was able to soften his temper, improve his manners and help him to support works of justice, mercy and charity. She assisted him with affairs of state, heard law suits, and influenced changes in the Scottish Church, seeking to reconcile differences between the various traditions. She accepted the martial pursuits of her husband Malcolm, but stirred his love and passion, so that he supported her in every endeavour. No doubt Turgot was able to aid the queen in daily living with a husband whose associates often had warlike attitudes.

Margaret loved reading, and Turgot was able to assist her,[26] following the gift by Bishop William of St-Calais to Durham monastery of a wide-ranging selection of devotional books. She possessed a command of eloquent words,[27] and her discussions with the prior are likely to have been on religious and social reform.

Early in 1092 Prior Turgot was moved to give permanence to the relationship between the Scottish throne and the Durham community. It was customary to agree conventions between bodies, particularly monasteries. A royal convention was made at Durham, whereby the monks of St Cuthbert agreed with Malcolm and Margaret to feed one poor man each day, and two on Maundy Thursday, and to say a collect for them at the Litany and at Mass. Further, both they and their sons and daughters would be partakers in all the good deeds performed to the glory of God, in masses, psalms, alms, vigils and prayers. On the days of the deaths of the king and queen, there would be thirty full offices for the dead. *Verba mea*[28] would be sung daily, and every priest would celebrate thirty masses and each of the others would sing ten psalters. Turgot asked brother William to enter the full details into the *Book of Life* kept at the cathedral.[29] The necrology of Durham recorded that the sovereigns' anniversary fell on 12 November,[30] although after Margaret's canonisation in 1250 her day was 21 April.

Margaret and Prior Turgot had similar interests. They were both builders. Having built the church of the Holy Trinity at Dunfermline, she reconstructed the ancient monastery at Iona, installed monks and provided an endowment.[31] She initiated the construction of St Regulus at St Andrews, to house the relics of Andrew the apostle. Its tower served as a landmark to guide pilgrims coming by sea. So many began coming from the south that Margaret was moved to provide hostels on both shores of the Firth of Forth, as well as a free ferry.[32] She built a chapel at Edinburgh Castle which became known as the little chapel of St Margaret, though the present building was by her youngest son, David (1124–53).[33]

In 1092 Margaret and Turgot were able to share the excitement of the opportunity to build a new cathedral at Durham, as the prior undertook a major part in the project. He knew the importance of maintaining a close relationship with the Scottish crown, and wished to invite the king and queen to lay the foundation stone. Events frustrated his desires.

Also in 1092 Rufus sent his army to annexe Cumbria, which annoyed Malcolm, who had occupied Cumbria from 1061 (see Chapter 1). He complained to the English king, who invited him to attend the royal court at Gloucester in August 1093.

Late in 1092 Margaret became very ill, mainly through lack of nourishment, and was soon to become bed-bound in Edinburgh Castle. In May 1093, Turgot records, "she therefore spoke to me privately, and began to relate her life to me in order; and to pour out rivers of tears at every word".[34] She made two requests of Turgot, "one that thou remember my soul in thy masses and prayers all thy life; the other, that thou take charge of my sons and daughters, and afford them love; and especially teach them, and never cease to teach them, to fear and love God".[35]

This was to be their last memorable conversation, and Margaret astounded Turgot with her ability to foretell future events. She predicted that the prior would enjoy a long life and her sons and daughters would be "elevated to the zenith of earthly dignity".[36] In 1093 the queen was well aware that the sons of Malcolm's first marriage were still living, and yet three sons of Margaret did become kings of Scotland, her elder daughter became queen of England, and her younger daughter countess of Boulogne and mother of an English queen. Who could hazard such predictions? Only by divine intervention could such visions have been fulfilled.

Malcolm left the queen in August 1093 and, accompanied by the queen's brother, Edgar the Ætheling, set out to see Rufus at Gloucester. They broke their journey at Durham where, on 11 August, Malcolm laid a foundation stone for the new cathedral, perhaps at the bidding of the queen.

Malcolm arrived at Gloucester on 24 August, but Rufus refused to meet him. Malcolm took the opportunity of visiting his daughter Edith at nearby Wilton, Wiltshire. In 1086 Margaret's sister, Christina, had become a nun at Romsey in Hampshire, and took her nieces with her to be educated as Norman ladies. Christina insisted that Edith wore a nun's habit and veil, an action that later nearly prevented her marriage to Henry I.[37] The girls then moved to the convent at Wilton, where Malcolm was furious to find her dressed once again as a nun. Without the soothing voice of Margaret, he tore off the habit and removed Edith. They returned to Scotland, which enabled Margaret to enjoy their company for a few months.

Later that year Malcolm set out on his last expedition to Northumbria, and was killed on 13 November 1093 near Alnwick, in an ambush set by Robert de Mowbray, earl of Northumbria. Malcolm's son and heir, Edward, was also killed. His son Edgar survived the ambush and carried the sad tidings to his mother at Edinburgh. Two peasants conveyed Malcolm's body in a cart to Tynemouth, probably on the order of de Mowbray, where it was buried. (Malcolm's son Alexander later re-interred it in Dunfermline Priory to lie with Margaret.)

Margaret had been ailing for six months, and on 13 November she seemed to anticipate the news, saying "to-day so great an evil has happened".[38] The queen entered the chapel to hear mass and asked for her 'black cross'. There was a delay in opening the casket and the queen groaned and said "we shall not be judged worthy to see again the holy Rood!"[39] When it was finally removed she embraced it, and kissed it. When her son arrived from the battle on 16 November, she asked how his father and brother were. Edgar was afraid of the effect the truth might have upon her in her weak state, and replied that they were well. She exclaimed "I know, my son, I know", then raising her hands towards heaven, she said, "I render praises and thanks to thee, almighty God, who hast willed that I should endure such anguish at my death; and to cleanse me, as I hope, by enduring it, from some stains of sin".[40] She ordered her chaplain to stand by her, and with the singing of psalms, her soul was commended to Christ. Margaret died that same day, her last words being "deliver me".[41]

The succession

Malcolm's brother, Donald Bán or Bane, claimed the throne of Scotland, and was elected under the Gaelic tradition of tanistry. By the custom of collateral succession, a brother had a stronger claim than a son. Donald laid siege to Edinburgh Castle, where the body of Margaret was being protected by her brother, Edgar the Ætheling. There was a single entrance to the castle which was closed, but their supporters knew of a postern gate on the west side of the castle, through which they escaped. Tradition recorded that "as they journeyed by land or by sea" across the Firth of Forth to Dunfermline, a thick mist surrounded them.[42] She was buried near the altar of the church which she and Malcolm had built.

The new king hated southerners "and drove out all the English who had been with King Malcolm".[43] This dislike of English ways led to a short-lived reaction against Margaret's reforms. Edgar the Ætheling took the queen's younger children to the court of William Rufus, calling at Durham en route. Turgot maintained a fatherly interest in the royal family—Edgar (19), Alexander (16), Edith (14), Mary (11) and David (9). This may have been Turgot's first meeting with Edith, for whom he wrote his Life of St Margaret, and to whom he dedicated it, after she had become queen of England (see Chapter 6).

Duncan II, Malcolm's son from his first marriage, seized the Scottish crown and reigned from May to November 1094. He granted to the Durham community lands south of the Forth estuary, including the hermit sanctuary of Tyninghame, East Lothian. Even when Donald Bane regained the throne, the absence of a warrior king like Malcolm could not stop these lands from being settled by Norman tenants. King William Rufus of England was able to exploit the situation.

Margaret's second son, Edmund, had sided with his uncle, Donald Bane, and was sent as a monk to the Cluniac monastery of Montacute in Somerset. Another son, Ethelred, had become earl of Fife and hereditary lay abbot of Dunkeld, but had already died. Margaret's next son, Edgar, was still in England at the royal court, and on 29 August 1095, issued a charter, giving the counties of Coldingham and Berwick to the community of St Cuthbert, while accepting the overlordship of King William Rufus throughout Lothian.[44] A charter of confirmation was drawn up in the cemetery of the church of St Cuthbert at Norham upon Tweed, in the presence of Bishop William and Prior Turgot.[45] The latter set up a cell or grange at Coldingham[46] to have oversight of these Durham lands. Turgot's archdeaconry now included Lothian and Carlisle.

In October 1097, Margaret's brother, Edgar the Ætheling, led an expedition from England to Scotland to put his nephew Edgar on the throne, with the support of the English king. On the way the Ætheling is said to have received a vision of St Cuthbert who directed him to obtain the saint's banner from Durham.[47] The two Edgars arrived and found that Turgot was expecting them, and the community presented Edgar with Cuthbert's banner.[48] If he bore this banner in battle, Cuthbert would be present and, after several battles in Scotland, victory was with Edgar.[49] Edgar reigned unmolested and secure in Scotland from 1097 until his death in 1107. Turgot's responsibilities, as promised to Margaret, were now over. He would not have been invited to Edgar's coronation, as Scottish kings were not crowned nor anointed, but inaugurated in a ceremony outside the church at Scone. Turgot must have been delighted when Edith married Henry I of England on 11 November 1100, becoming Queen Matilda.

Turgot the bishop

When Alexander (1107–24) succeeded his brother as king of Scotland, he found that the see of St Andrews had been vacant since 1093. He asked Henry I of England to appoint Turgot to be bishop of St Andrews and primate of Scotland. He had known Turgot from his childhood, his mother having requested the prior to look after his education on her death. He would have been aware of the support Turgot had given to Queen Margaret, and of his work as both prior and archdeacon of Durham. He wanted Turgot to help reform the Scottish church and bring it into line with the rest of western Christendom.

For some thirty years Turgot had maintained regular contact with the Scottish royal family. He had been in a favoured position as Queen Margaret's spiritual adviser. The kings north of the border accepted him as a true friend, and gave permanence to their relationship with the community of St Cuthbert. Turgot constantly had to acknowledge the kings of two countries, and saw more of the kings of Scotland than those of England. Prince Alexander had been present at the translation of St Cuthbert in 1104 and his name features prominently in Durham's *Book of Life,* which recorded names of benefactors.[50]

The see of St Andrews had been subject to control by the archbishops of York since 1072, when Bishop Fothad II professed subjection to York "by counsel and command of Malcolm king of Scots and Queen Margaret",[51] though no doubt it was the queen that had wished the agreement. Turgot continued to maintain the supremacy of York over St Andrews, whereas King Alexander favoured the more remote control of Canterbury, following his mother's preference when founding the royal monastery at Dunfermline. The king refused to endorse the 1072 agreement, and wished Turgot to work for independence from the control of the archbishop of York.

When Turgot arrived at St Andrews, following his consecration in August 1109, he found a situation far removed from his accustomed routine. There was no cathedral as such, and it must have been a daunting thought to begin again without the inspiration and financial backing of William of St-Calais. There was a primitive reliquary church, which may have served as a cathedral. Pilgrims had begun to worship at the reliquary of St Andrew towards the end of the eleventh century, and Queen Margaret had always supported the Culdees there. The Culdees were a distinct community at St Andrews, but living in families and following their own traditional forms of worship. Turgot found it impossible to practise Benedictine monasticism where there were no dedicated monks and where there had been no bishop for sixteen years. The Culdees occupied many of the old Scottish monasteries, none of which had adopted the Benedictine Rule.

Turgot soon found it impossible to reconcile the various factions—the king, the archbishopric of York, the Culdees—all attempting to make him abandon the truths he had known. In addition, some aspects of the practices criticised in the 1090s by Queen Margaret were still unresolved. King Alexander sent messengers to Pope Paschal II, asking him to write to Turgot about these matters: the four seasons of fasting (Ember-days), the giving of the Eucharist to children, and the making of confession to priests. Paschal replied in two letters, a general one to the clergy and laity, telling them to commit themselves to Turgot's advice—"our fellow bishop, whom we have heard to be among the wiser among you"[52]—and a personal letter to Turgot, referring him to rulings of the fifth-century popes Calixtus I, Leo I and Gelasius I, to be found in a book of excerpts from canon law that he sent with the letter. These letters were copied onto some blank pages in a copy of Archbishop Lanfranc's canon law collection, formerly belonging to Durham Priory.[53] The letters are dated 26 June and 18 August respectively, the first sent from Rome, the second from the pope's summer residence at Civita Castellana in the hills to the north of Rome, the change of venue doubtless accounting for the time lapse. The year is not stated, but must have been 1112, 1113 or 1114.

Perhaps it was in response to these letters that Turgot proposed to go to Rome to consult Pope Paschal II in person—he may even have contemplated retiring there—"he prepared to go to Rome, where he could pass his life under the counsel and advice of the lord Pope Paschal".[54] This led to a quarrel with King Alexander, who forbade him to go. The journey to Rome was long and dangerous, and quite unsuitable for a man of Turgot's age.[55] Possibly Alexander also considered that such a journey would delay the changes he wanted introduced, already long overdue because of the deferment of Turgot's consecration for a year due to his obedience to York.

Turgot must have felt further abandoned in 1114 when Thomas II of York died and the new archbishop-elect found himself in opposition to the archbishop of Canterbury and the king of England. The tussle between King Alexander, Archbishop Anselm and Bishop Ranulf Flambard of Durham, over the metropolitan supremacy of York in connection with the bishopric of St Andrews, continued for many years. Turgot found it increasingly difficult to support earthly kings while living for Christ, his spiritual king.

He would have found some respite in 1113, when the king's youngest brother, David, married Matilda, daughter and heiress of Waltheof, earl of Huntingdon and

Northumberland. Turgot is bound to have attended the wedding. David had also inherited from King Edgar extensive territories south of the Forth. In 1113 David introduced thirteen monks from Tiron, France, and settled them at Selkirk, though they moved to Kelso in 1128. (It was also in 1128 that David invited Augustinian canons from Merton, in Surrey, to found Holyrood Abbey in Edinburgh, to house his mother's 'Holy Rood'.[56] David became king of Scotland in 1124.)

In 1114 King Alexander had the Culdee monastery at Scone in Gowrie rebuilt, and the church was dedicated to the Holy Trinity by Turgot.[57] The church was founded in honour of Alexander's victory over the men of Moray. Augustinian canons were invited to come from Nostell, Yorkshire.[58]

The dedication by Turgot was one of his last public engagements. His health broke down under the anxieties that he was enduring. He decided to seek healing at St Cuthbert's shrine. In 1115 Turgot "received licence to stay for a while at Durham",[59] where he died.

Alexander later sought the promotion of Eadmer, the great literary leader at Canterbury, to replace Turgot. Eadmer was appointed in 1120. The *scholastici* turned out to welcome the bishop-elect.[60] No doubt they had done the same for Turgot.

▲ *St Serf's Inch on Loch Leven, by Thomas Hodge, from Lang p. 16.*

The Culdees (*céli-dé*) and St Andrews

The name Culdee derives from *céli-dé*, which is the Irish Gaelic for 'servant of God', and the name was given to Irish hermits. They followed the Tallaght rule based on the teachings of their founder Maelruain but took no monastic vows. During their first year of training novices did not take communion.

When they arrived in Scotland, via Iona, the name became *kele dei* and the kings of the Picts were early associated with them. About 845 King Brude, son of Dergard, gave the island, since called St Serf's Inch on Loch Leven, "to God, St Servan and the Culdee hermits".[61] The kings of the Picts and of Scotland regularly gave grants of land and immunities to the *céli-dé*. Constantine mac Aeda, king of Scotland 900–943, exchanged his crown for a monk's cowl, and became the abbot of the Culdees of St Andrews.[62] He upheld church rights on the 'Hill of Belief' at Scone in 906, with Bishop Kellach in attendance, and St Andrews became the centre of the Scottish Church. Thereafter, the monastery site of Kilrimont became known as St Andrews, with a reliquary church which housed bones of the saint. These may have been within the existing sarcophagus which dates from the end of the tenth century.

St Andrew the apostle was martyred in about AD 60 at Patras, Greece, on the orders of the Roman governor of Achaea. In vengeance, in 345 Constantius sacked Patras and took the saint's body to Constantinople. One legend says that some of his bones were hidden by St Regulus at Patras, who took them to Scotland, setting up a shrine at Kilrimont, where a monastery may have been founded by King Óengus mac Fergusa of the Picts (729–761).[63]

About 1090, Queen Margaret of Scotland provided a free ferry (Queensferry) to transport pilgrims across the Firth of Forth on their way to and from St Andrews. In 1093 Fothad mac Maolmhicheil, the last of the Celtic bishops of St Andrews, died and the diocese was without a bishop for fourteen years. The Culdees claimed that they had a right to elect a new bishop but this was disallowed by Rome. In 1100 Pope Paschal II instructed the Scottish bishops to show obedience to the archbishop of York, and from this time the bishops sought to gain their independence.

Queen Margaret's son Alexander became king of Scotland in January 1107, and requested that Henry I of England should assign the vacant bishopric of St Andrews to Turgot, prior of Durham, and biographer of Margaret. There was a delay in filling the vacancy which could not proceed until the archbishop elect of York had been consecrated. This was completed in August 1109. Turgot found it difficult to be the leader of the Scottish church and to be obedient to the archbishop. The Culdees continued in their traditional ways, while Turgot was used to a disciplined life following the Rule of St Benedict.

Following the death of Turgot in 1115 Eadmer, a monk of Canterbury, was elected bishop of St Andrews in 1120, but he found the rivalry between York and Canterbury intolerable and resigned in 1121 before he was consecrated.

The next bishop was Robert who had been a canon of St Oswald's Augustinian priory of Nostell, Yorkshire. Elected in 1124, he decided to construct a new reliquary church of St Regulus, as he had access to superb masons from Yorkshire. He was consecrated in 1127 when the new church was also dedicated. This became the cathedral church of St Andrews, with a tall bell-tower calling the faithful to prayer.

In 1144 Bishop Robert founded an Augustinian monastery at St Andrews and gave churches and land to support a new community, some of which had been Culdee possessions.[64] To the Culdees at St Serf's Inch on Loch Leven, the bishop gave a choice. They could choose "to live canonically and peacefully under the new [Augustinian] canons, and remain in the island", or be expelled. In Aberdeenshire at Monymusk he converted a Culdee community into a small Augustinian priory under the bishop's protection.

The thirteen Culdees living at St Andrews continued to use their own church of Blessed Mary on the Rock and also retained a voice in the election of any new bishop. By 1150 most had joined the Augustinian community, and the church of St Regulus became the priory church. Bishop Robert fully accepted the desire of King David of Scotland that, as chief bishop of Scotland, he rendered no obedience to the archbishop of York, while the voices of the bishops grew louder for independence.

They had traditional memories of the dispute at the Synod of Whitby in 664, when it was reasoned by King Oswy that St Peter, with the keys of the kingdom, was to be considered more important than St Columba of Iona. The Scottish bishops felt that, with the protection of St Andrew, brother of St Peter, and the possession of his relics,[65] they were capable of administering their own affairs. St Andrew now displaced St Columba as the patron saint of Scotland.

The Culdees were still active in 1147, when Pope Eugenius III gave instructions that, when vacancies of prebends arose from death, etc., they were to be bestowed upon Augustinian canons in place of the Culdees. [66]

Bishop Robert (1127–59) had a fruitful tenure as bishop, but was not able to build a new cathedral. This was begun by his successor in 1160, but was not completed under the bishoprics of Arnold, or his successors Richard, or John. Bishop John was consecrated on 15 June 1180, and his successor, Hugh, went to Rome in 1188 to discuss the primacy, but died there, probably of malaria.

In 1192 Pope Celestine III issued a bull, *cum universi,* which established a special relationship of the Scottish church to the papacy. Nine dioceses were listed in Scotland, plus the newly created see of Argyll.

CHAPTER 8

The Death of Turgot

Turgot left St Andrews in June 1115 and arrived in Monkwearmouth on 28 June on his way to Durham. He was ill, but was determined to celebrate a (last) mass where he had first been clothed with the monastic habit some forty years previously.[1] He then set out for Durham and "there taking to his bed, his end was preceded by febrile attacks, sometimes low, sometimes acute, and this for two months and four days".[2] He knew his end was near and he was thankful that he was able to die near the body of St Cuthbert.

Thurstan, archbishop-elect of York, visited him at Durham, wishing to learn as much as possible from Turgot and his experiences. This was an opportunity for Thurstan to learn of the subtleties of Anglo-Scottish relations, and was one of his first engagements as archbishop-elect. Bishop Ranulf Flambard was with him.[3] Thurstan had been nominated to be archbishop on 15 August 1114, but he was not consecrated until Sunday 19 October 1119 in Reims Cathedral at the hands of Pope Callixtus, and he received the pallium on 1 November 1119. King Henry I forbade him to return to England, but relented in 1120. Thurstan had been ordained deacon in December 1114, and received priest's orders at the hands of Ranulf Flambard at Bayeux on Whit Sunday 1115. Thurstan and Flambard probably journeyed to Durham to meet Turgot in July 1115. Turgot "rejoiced extremely at Thurstan's promotion and his visit and put himself in his hands recognising him as his father and metropolitan".[4]

Symeon says that Turgot died 31 March 1115 (*ii kal Aprilis*),[5] but this is clearly an error, as he also records his arrival at Durham in June 1115. The correct date was 31 August 1115, as found in a letter of King Alexander to the archbishop of Canterbury: "We inform you, kindest father, that the bishop of the church of St Andrew the apostle, master Turgot, on the second before the Kalends of September departed from the world. Wherefore we are greatly afflicted by the loss of so great consolation".[6] This date agrees with Turgot's entry in the *Liber vitae* on *ii kal Septembris*.[7] He died with the words of Psalm 76:2 on his lips: "His dwelling is in peace and his habitation in Sion".[8] Although he was never bishop of Durham, Turgot was buried in the chapter house, between the graves of bishops Walcher and William of St-Calais.[9] A long, narrow, grave-cover was prepared of freestone and an inscription made: ✠ TURGOTUS EPISCO.[10]

Turgot's mortuary roll

At some time after his death a mortuary roll was prepared and circulated to religious houses in England and northern France, to announce his death and to elicit prayers for his soul. Two fragments of this roll were later used as the rear end-leaves of a manuscript containing a copy of William of Jumièges' *Gesta Normannorum ducum*, or *Deeds of the Dukes of Normandy* (a work which Turgot had mentioned in his *Life of St Margaret*).[11] Now in the British Library,[12] this manuscript was written at

Durham for, and partly by, Turgot's contemporary, the cantor and historian Symeon of Durham. The present binding with these end-leaves probably took place in the fifteenth century.[13]

If Symeon was already cantor in 1115, he would have been responsible for preparing the roll, according to the *Constitutiones* of Archbishop Lanfranc, which list among the cantor's duties "to supervise the letters sent out to ask for prayers for the dead brethren".[14] He would also have prepared the accompanying encyclical letter, describing the life of the deceased. This has not survived, so it is fortunate that Symeon recorded in some detail the key points in Turgot's life in his *Historia regum*.[15]

The fragments of Turgot's mortuary roll are believed to represent the oldest surviving mortuary roll of English origin, though a few earlier ones of continental origin survived long enough to be transcribed, one reaching 253 religious communities, of which 63 were in England.[16] Each house visited added the name of their community to the roll, and most of them added a prayer, or even a verse. Both sides of the roll were used for this purpose.

Only ten such subscriptions or *tituli* survive from the fragments of Turgot's roll, and not all of those are complete or fully legible. The communities represented were the cathedral church of Notre-Dame, Laon; the Benedictine abbey of St-Vincent the Martyr, Laon; the collegiate church of Holy Cross, Waltham; an unidentified religious house dedicated to the Blessed Virgin Mary; a church dedicated to St Laud, presumably that at Angers; the Benedictine abbey of St-Laumer, Blois; a religious house dedicated to St Florentius, perhaps the Benedictine abbey of St-Florent-lès-Saumur; an unknown convent; the Benedictine abbey of St-Quentin-en-l'Île, Saint-Quentin; and the Benedictine abbey of St-Prix, Saint-Quentin. No doubt other places were visited, but their tituli have not survived. The convents represented here were widespread, covering the counties of Anjou, Blois, Touraine and Vermandois, as well as Essex, so the roll would have been in active circulation for a considerable period, perhaps some twelve to eighteen months.

For three of these ten, only the heading naming the community survives, being at the bottom of a fragment. Another, at the top of a fragment, has just the final four lines of text, severely rubbed and barely legible. Most of the entries start with the prayer "may his soul rest in peace" [*anima eius requiescat in pace*], some are extended to include "and the souls of all the faithful departed" [*et anime omnium fidelium defunctorum*]. Four request prayers for named deceased brethren [*orate pro nostris . . .*], many of whom can be identified from other sources. Four entries incorporate some form of elegiac verse, to the effect that praise is futile, and prayers will be of greater benefit to the deceased. Turgot is named only in the verse from the abbey of Saint-Quentin-en-l'Île, so it is fortunate that this entry has survived, if only in part.

Turgot translated

According to *The Chronicle of Lanercost*, on 4 June 1284 those digging a grave in the chapter house for Bishop Robert de Coquina accidentally broke into Turgot's tomb. "By this time he had lain in the depth of the earth eight score and nine years, yet he was not only found entire in his body, but also in his vestments, the diggers having accidentally broken the case containing his pastoral staff. Having therefore shown the unchanged remains of this venerable man to several persons, they filled in the place with the earth that had been thrown out, and prepared elsewhere a grave befitting such remains".[17] Bishop Robert's tomb was in the eastern apse of the chapter house, and was excavated in 1874.[18]

Postscript

In 1868 J. Hodgson Hinde dismissed Turgot's achievements as follows: "His tenure of the priorate was unmarked by any important events, if we except the rebuilding of the church of St. Cuthbert, a work more immediately due to the bishop, but to which he contributed his assistance, and the translation of St. Cuthbert's remains. His subsequent career as Bishop of St Andrew's was as unsatisfactory as his earlier experience of the same country during his residence at Melrose".[19]

The evidence suggests that Turgot's role in the building of the cathedral was more important than Hinde realised, and that he played a key role in the political, social and ecclesiastical hierarchy of Durham and the north-east.

The life of Turgot was clearly of great importance to the community of St Cuthbert in many spheres—in his role as one of the founders of the monastic revival

▼ *Durham Cathedral: the east end of the chapter house in 1795. Another sketch by John Carter from Greenwell* Drawings PLATE II.

in Northumbria in the 1070s; in building up and maintaining a thriving monastery, being its prior for over twenty-two years; in being responsible for the whole bishopric in the bishops' absences over twelve years; in giving comfort and guidance to the Scottish royal family; and in safeguarding the northern territories for the kings of England by maintaining such relationships. In 1091, when William Rufus received a delegation from Durham, he acknowledged Turgot's importance when he humbly rose to greet him.[20]

To Turgot, the service of St Cuthbert represented the abiding importance of the cathedral, but the absence of the bishop on government business meant that this sometimes had to be subservient to the needs of administering the diocese and maintaining good relationships with the kings of England and the people of the monastery's lands. They were their own folk, but subject to the earls of Bamburgh in the north and to the rulers of York to the south. They feared armies from the north and the south.

During Turgot's priorate, the bishops of Durham were formidable royal officials, unable to devote much time to the community of St Cuthbert. There were always pressures to concentrate on other matters—the demands of the royal administration; ecclesiastical reform and canon law; the settling of Norman knights on both sides of the border—but Turgot was always ready to step into the breach. Bishop Walcher was chosen by William I in 1071 to control the northern frontier. He started work on the cloister, but perhaps his most significant contribution towards the building of the present cathedral is the encouragement he gave to Turgot in becoming a monk of the Cuthbert fraternity. In 1082 William of St-Calais followed as bishop. He was part of the monastic tradition, while serving the king as chamberlain. He was certainly a formidable person, who knew what he wanted and who inspired others to want what he wanted. The third was Ranulf Flambard, a Norman who desired to make a name for himself and who had plenty of ability.

The biggest disappointment in Turgot's life must have been the realisation that he would not live to see the completion of every aspect of his dream—the fully developed plan with a roof over the nave. But Turgot was very lucky. He was present at the moment that Bishop William gave the go-ahead for rebuilding the cathedral, and he was present at the completion of the presbytery and the shrine of St Cuthbert. He may have been the only person to have seen the construction of the cathedral from the laying of a foundation stone in 1093 to the building of the nave walls in 1115. How many other men have had their dream shattered by the rejection of a 'too revolutionary design', the running out of funds, the onset of war, plague or sickness? There were thousands with great talent who never had such an opportunity.

When we think of the millions of pilgrims, local citizens, worshippers and tourists who have been blessed with divine love within those hallowed walls, we should spare a thought for a Lincolnshire lad who made it all possible.

Turgot wrote that Queen Margaret chose him as a close friend, "not because there was anything good in me, but because she thought that there was".[21] He spent his life with saints and would have been known by them. He himself was never numbered with the saints, not because there were no saintly qualities in his life, but perhaps because men thought that there were none.

Turgot's *Life of St Margaret Queen of Scotland*

*Translation by Alan Orr Anderson, reproduced
courtesy of James Sandeman and Shaun Tyas.*[1]

For the excellently honourable and honourably excellent queen of the English, Matilda, T., servant of the servants of St Cuthbert, [implores] the benefit of peace and health in the present [life]; and in the future [life] the benefit of all benefits.

Requesting, you have commanded, and in commanding have requested, me to give you in writing an account of the God-pleasing life of your mother, of venerable memory; since you have heard it very often proclaimed, with the concordant praises of many speakers. You said, indeed, that I was especially to be trusted in this, because you had heard that, by reason of my great friendship with her, I was in great part familiar with her secret thoughts.

I gladly embrace these commands and these wishes; in embracing them I revere them much; in revering them, I congratulate you, in that, being appointed queen of the Angles by the king of the angels, you desire not only to hear of the life of the queen your mother, who ever aspired to the realm of angels, but also to have it constantly before you in writing: so that, although you knew but little your mother's face, you may have more fully the knowledge of her virtues.

But although my will is ready to perform the commands laid upon me, yet, I confess, I have no fitness for it; for this subject is greater than is my ability [to describe it] in writing or in speech. And thus my feelings are twofold, and I am drawn by them in contrary directions. I dread to obey, because of the magnitude of the affair; but because of the authority of her who commands, and for the sake of the memory of her who is the theme, I dare not refuse. But although I am unable to describe so great a matter in a manner worthy of it, yet I ought to relate as much as I can; because this is required both by love for her, and by your command. The Holy Spirit's favour, which gave to her the faculty of her virtues, will afford me aid, I hope, in relating them. "The Lord will give words to those that preach the gospel"; and again, "Open thy mouth, and I will fill it." Nor indeed can he lack words who believes in the Word: for "the word was in the beginning, and the word was God."

To begin with, then, I desire both you and others through you to know that if I attempt to tell all that I know should be proclaimed of her, I shall be thought in praising your mother to flatter you, because of the loftiness of your royal rank: but far be it from my grey hairs to involve the virtues of so great a woman in a charge of falsehood; in expounding them, God be witness and judge, I profess that I add nothing to that which is; but in order that they appear not incredible, I pass over in silence many things: lest, in the words of the orator, I be said to adorn the crow in colours of the swan.

Chapter 1: How Margaret, becoming a queen, preserved in her works the beauty of her name.

Many, as we have read, have had the origin of their name in some quality of mind; so that the word showed some fitness with such grace as they had received. So Peter [was named] from the rock, Christ, because of the firmness of his faith; so John, which means "grace of God," for contemplation of the Godhead and the privilege of God's love; and the sons of Zebedee were called Boanerges, that is "sons of thunder," because of the thunder of their proclamation of the gospel. This happened also in the case of this woman of virtue; for she excelled in the greater beauty of her soul the prettiness that she bore in her name. She was called Margaret, and in her faith and works she was held as a precious pearl in God's sight. And so the pearl—yours, mine; ours; nay, Christ's; and because Christ's, so much the more ours—has now left us, being taken to the Lord. The pearl, I repeat, has been taken from the dungheap of this world; and glows now, set in the diadem of the eternal king. No one will doubt this, when he has heard, a little further on, of her life and her life's end.

When I recollect her conversations with me, seasoned with the salt of wisdom; when I think of the tears that her heart's remorse had caused; when I review her soberness, and the well-ordered nature of her life; when I remember her affability and prudence; in my grief I rejoice; and, rejoicing, grieve. I rejoice because she has passed to the God whom she had longed for; I grieve because I do not rejoice with her in heaven. For her, I repeat, I rejoice, because she now sees what she had believed in, the good things of the Lord in the land of the living; but for myself, I grieve, since I am impelled (while I suffer the miseries of mortal life in this land of the dead) to cry daily, "Wretched man that I am, who shall deliver me from the body of this death?"

Chapter 2: How from noble ancestry she drew her pedigree.

Since, then, I am to speak of the nobility of mind which she had in Christ, it seems that something should be prefixed of the other nobility also, in which she was distinguished according to the world. Her grandfather had been King Edmund, who, because he was vigorous in fighting and invincible against his foes, had earned the distinction of a name from the excellence of his valour; for he was named in the English tongue what in Latin is called *Ferreum-latus*,[2] and his brother (by his father; not by his mother) had been that most pious and gentle [Edward], who had shown himself the father of his country; and as in some sense a second Solomon, that is, a peaceful man, he had protected the kingdom rather with peace than with arms. He bore a mind triumphant over anger, contemptuous of greed, and wholly free from pride. Nor was this strange; because just as from his ancestors he acquired the glory of his rank, so he acquired also honourable life, as by a certain hereditary right; he being descended from grandfathers not only most noble, but also very religious: Edgar, king of the English, and Richard, count of the Normans. Of these, to tell briefly how great Edgar was in the world, and of what merit in Christ, it was foreshown that he was to be both a king and a lover of peace and justice. For at his birth, the blessed Dunstan heard holy angels rejoicing in the sky, and singing with great rejoicing: "Let there be peace, let there be gladness in the church of the English, so long as the boy now born holds the kingdom, and Dunstan runs with [him] the way of mortal life." Also Richard, the father of Emma, Edward's mother, had lustre worthy of so great a nephew, being a man vigorous in all things, and to be praised by every crier. None of his ancestors was either more fortunate in the honour of the country, or more zealous in the love of religion. He was surrounded with the greatest wealth; but, another David in spirit, he was as the poorest. He was appointed lord over the peoples; yet he was the humblest servant of the servants of Christ. Among the other things that he had done as a memorial of his religious devotion, the devout worshipper of Christ had built the noble monastery of Fécamp; in which he had often been accustomed to dwell with the monks—a secular in costume, but a monk in action—and in silence to place food before them at meal-times, and to serve them with drink; in order that, according to the Scripture, the greater he was the more he should humble himself in all things. He that wishes to know more fully of the works of [Richard's] magnificence and virtues, let him read the *Gesta Normannorum*, which contains his acts also.

The grandson Edward was in no way degenerate from these ancestors, of so great glory and excellence: as has been said before, he was brother (by his father only) of King Edmund, whose son's daughter, Margaret, with the glory of her merits greatly adorns the glorious line of her ancestors.

Chapter 3: How she began in her earliest youth; and, when raised up to honour, did not delight in honour.

While she still flourished in early youth she began to lead a life of soberness, and to love God above all things; to occupy herself in the study of divine readings, and to employ her mind upon them with delight. She was endowed with keen acuteness of intellect, to understand any matter; with much tenacity of memory, to retain it; with gracious facility of words, to express it.

While thus she meditated day and night upon the law of the Lord, and like another Mary sitting at the Lord's feet delighted to hear his word, she was united in marriage with the most powerful king of the Scots, Malcolm, King Duncan's son, by the will of her relatives more than by her own; or rather, by God's disposition. But although she was compelled to have to do with the things that belong to this world, yet she scorned to adhere in desire to the world's affairs. She delighted more in good works than in the possession of riches. Out of temporal goods she prepared for herself eternal rewards, because she had placed her heart in heaven, where her treasure was. And because she sought chiefly the kingdom of God and his justice, the Omnipotent's bountiful favour gave her in abundance honours and riches.

Everything that was fitting [for her to do] was done under the prudent queen's rule: the laws of the realm were adjusted by her counsel; divine religion was furthered by her industry; the people rejoiced in the prosperity of commerce. Nothing was firmer than her faith, more constant than her countenance, more enduring than her patience, more important than her advice, juster than her opinion, pleasanter than her conversation.

Chapter 4: How in the place of her marriage she erected a church, and with what zeal she caused decorations of churches to be prepared; and with how great temperance she governed herself and her [servants].

After she had risen to the summit of honour, she presently erected an eternal monument to her name and religiousness, in the place where her wedding had been celebrated.³ She built a noble church there in honour of the holy Trinity, with threefold purpose of salvation; that is to say, for the redemption of the king's soul and of her own, and in order to obtain for her children prosperity in this life and the life to come. This church she decorated with various kinds of adornments; among them are known to have been several vessels of pure and solid gold, for the sacred ministry of the altar. This I might know with the greater certainty, because for a long time I myself there received charge of them all, at the queen's command. She placed there also a cross of incomparable value, bearing the Saviour's image; she had had it all overlaid with purest gold and silver, with jewels set here and there between: even today it proves clearly to beholders the devoutness of her faith.

Similarly also she has left signs of her faith and holy devotion in all the other churches; for instance, the church of St Andrews, as may be seen today, preserves a most elegant image of a crucifix, which she herself erected there. Her chamber was never empty of these things (that is, of the things that pertained to the adornment of divine service); it seemed to be a kind of workshop, so to speak, of celestial art. There were always seen copes for the cantors, chasubles, stoles, altar-cloths, and other priestly vestments, and decorations for the church. Some were being prepared by the artist's hand; others, finished, were kept as being worthy of admiration.

For these labours women were appointed who, being noble by birth and approved for sober manners, were adjudged worthy to enter the queen's service. There was no access of men-folk to these women, except when [the queen] herself permitted them to enter with her, upon her occasional visits to them. They had no unseemly intimacy with men, never any impudent levity. For the queen possessed so great pleasantness with severity, that all who were in her service, men and women, both loved her with fear, and feared her with love: so that in her presence none of them would have dared even to use a low word, let alone to do anything detestable. For she repressed in herself every vice, and was very serious in rejoicing, very upright in anger. She never broke into loud laughter with immoderate mirth, never fell into fury when she was enraged. At times she was wroth with others' sins, but with her own sins always, with that praiseworthy, ever justice-loving anger which the psalmist taught we should have, when he said, "Be ye angry, and sin not."

Her whole life, ordered by extreme control of discretion, was a pattern of virtue. Her speech was seasoned with the salt of wisdom; her silence was full of good meditations. Her character so agreed with the soberness of her manners, that one might have believed her born for nobility of life alone. To express much in few words, in everything that she said, in everything that she did, she showed that her mind was set upon heavenly things.

Chapter 5: [How] her sons were honourably [brought up].
She gave no less care to her sons than to herself, so that they should be brought up with every attention, and instructed as far as possible in honourable ways. And because she knew that it is written, "he who spares the rod hates his son", she had directed the steward of the household to restrain them himself with threats and whippings whenever they erred in infantile naughtiness, as is young children's way. Through this scrupulous care of their mother, as children they excelled in uprightness of manners many who were more advanced in age: they were ever kind and peaceful among themselves, and the younger everywhere showed honour to

the elder. Thus even at the celebration of mass, when they went forward after their parents to the offering, the younger by no means ventured to go before the elder; but in the order of age the elder used to precede the younger.

She took great pains, bringing [her sons] very often before her, to teach them, as far as their age could understand, of Christ and of Christ's faith, and to exhort them always to fear him. "Fear the Lord, my sons," she said, "since those that fear him shall have no lack. And if you love him, O my children, he gives you in return both prosperity in this life, and eternal felicity with all the saints."

This was their mother's desire, this her exhortation, this her prayer with tears, by day and night, for her children, that they should acknowledge their creator in faith which works by love; acknowledging, should worship him; and worshipping, should love him in everything and above everything; and by loving him should reach the glory of the heavenly kingdom.

Chapter 6: [How] zealous she was in reading; [seek]ing in this not her own salvation only, but others' also.

It is not to be marvelled at that a queen who was always governed by the wisest instruction of holy scripture should rule herself and her people with wise government. For (what I used to admire much in her) among the discords of law-suits, among manifold cares of state, she applied herself with wonderful zeal to divine reading; concerning which she very often discussed even minute points with the most learned men who were present. But just as none present among them was of deeper intelligence than she, so none was clearer in eloquence. And so it very often occurred that the teachers themselves went away from her much wiser than they had been when they came.

She had in fact a great religious greed for holy volumes, and her intimate friendship and friendly intimacy with me compelled me to exert myself very much in procuring them for her.

In all this she sought not her own salvation only, but also that of others; and first of all, God helping her, she had made the king himself very readily inclined to works of justice, mercy, alms, and other virtues. He learned from her also to prolong vigils of the night frequently, with prayer; he learned by her exhortation and example to pray to God with groaning of heart, and shedding of tears. I confess I marvelled at this great miracle of God's mercy, when sometimes I saw so great application of the king to prayer; and during prayer so great remorse, in a layman's breast. He was fearful of offending her in any way, a queen of such venerable life, since he perceived that Christ truly dwelt in her heart; but rather hastened in all things to obey very quickly her wishes and prudent counsellings; he too to reject the same things that she had rejected, and for love of her to love the things that she had loved. Thus, although ignorant of letters, he used often to handle and gaze on the books in which she had been accustomed either to pray or read; and when he had heard from her which of them was dearest to her, to hold it dearer too, to kiss it and fondle it often. Sometimes also he called in a goldsmith, and gave orders that the book should be adorned with gold and jewels; and the king himself used to bring it back, decorated, to the queen, as a mark of devotion.

Chapter 7: How much honour and glory she conferred upon the kingdom of the Scots.

Also this noblest jewel of royal race made the magnificence of royal honour much more magnificent for the king; and she conferred very great glory and honour upon all the nobles of the kingdom, and their attendants. For she had caused merchants to come by land and sea from various regions, and to bring very many precious wares that were still unknown there. As an instance of this, the natives compelled by the queen bought clothing of different colours, and various ornaments of dress. Arrayed at her instigation in different refinements of dress, they bore themselves so that they seemed to have been in some sense reformed by this elegance.

She instituted also more ceremonious service of the king, so that when he walked or rode he was surrounded with great honour by many troops; and this with such discipline that, wherever they went, none of them was permitted to despoil anyone, nor did any of them dare to oppress or to injure countrymen or poor men in any way. She multiplied also the adornments of the royal palace, so that not only was it resplendent with various adornment of silken cloths; but even the whole house glittered with gold and silver. The vessels in which food and drink were brought to the king and the nobles of the realm were either made of gold or silver, or overlaid with gold or silver.

All this she had done not because she delighted in the honour of the world, but because she was compelled to perform what kingly dignity demanded of her. For while she went clad in costly elegance, as befitted a queen, like another Esther she spurned in her mind all ornaments, and regarded herself but as dust and ashes underneath her jewels and gold; and indeed always took greatest pains to preserve humility amid so great exultation of rank. She checked all the more easily every swelling of pride that arises from worldly honours, because consciousness of the transient nature of frail life had never left her. She had ever in her thoughts that saying which thus describes the hazardous state of human life: "Man, of woman born, lives for a short time, and is sated with many miseries; as a flower he comes forth, and is crushed, and like a shadow he flies, and never continues in the same state." And she constantly revolved in her mind the words of blessed James the apostle, saying, "What is our life? It is smoke, appearing for a little while; and afterwards it will be quenched." And because, as the scripture says, "Blessed is the man who is ever fearful," the venerable queen avoided sin so much the more easily, because trembling and in fear she always held up before the mind's eyes the appointed day of judgement. And therefore she frequently asked me not to hesitate to rebuke her in private, and point out to her whatever I perceived to be blameworthy either in her words or her deeds. When I did this more rarely and less warmly than she wished, she was harsh with me; she told me that I was sleeping, and as it were neglecting her. "Let the just man reprove me" she said, "in mercy and chide me; and let not the oil of the sinner" (that is, flattery) "anoint my head. For wounds inflicted by a friend are better than a flattering enemy's kisses." Thus speaking, for the advancement of virtue she courted the rebuke that any other might have considered an insult.

Chapter 8: How she [corrected] the things that they did contrary to the faith and the custom of the holy Church, and [induced them to observe] the rules.

While the queen, religious and worthy of God, was with mind, and words, and deeds, advancing to the heavenly country, she invited others also to go with her upon the perfect way, so that they might be able to attain to true bliss. When she saw a bad man, she exhorted him to become good: a good man, to be better; better, to endeavour to be best: since zeal for the house of God, which is the church, consumed her, glowing with apostolic faith. Hence also she laboured to eradicate wholly the illegalities that had sprung up in [the church]. For when she saw that many things were done in that nation contrary to the rule of the true faith and the holy custom of the universal church, she appointed many councils, in order by Christ's gift to bring back the wanderers, in whatever way she could, to the path of truth. Of these councils the principal is well known to have been that in which she alone, with very few of her supporters, fought for three days with "the sword of the spirit, that is to say the word of God," against the defenders of perverted custom. You would have thought that another Helen sat there; because as [Helen] had formerly confuted the Jews with verdicts from the scriptures, so now did this queen also confute the erring. But in this conflict the king himself continued as her chief helper, most ready to say and to do whatever she bade in this affair. And since he knew the tongue of the Angles perfectly, as well as his own, he was in this council a most careful interpreter for both sides.

Thus the queen, after making the introductory statement that those who served one God in one faith with the catholic church ought not to differ from that church in any new or foreign institutions, made her first proposition, that they did not legally keep the fast of Lent; because they were accustomed to begin it, not (with the holy church universally) [upon the fourth day of the week[4]] on the beginning of the fast, but on the second day of the [following] week. They said in reply: "The fast that we hold, we keep for six weeks, according to the authority of the gospel, which describes the fast of Christ." She replied: "You differ in this widely from the gospel: for we read there that the Lord fasted for forty days, and it is obvious that you do not. Since six Sundays are deducted during the six weeks, it is clear that only thirty-six days remain for the fast. Therefore it is clear that you do not keep the fast by authority of the gospel, for forty days; but for thirty-six. It remains for you therefore to begin to fast with us four days before the beginning of Lent, if you wish to preserve abstinence for the number of forty days, according to the Lord's example: otherwise you alone resist the authority of the Lord himself, and the tradition of the entire holy church."

They were overcome by this clear statement of the truth, and thenceforth began to commence the celebration of the sacred fast according to the custom everywhere of holy church.

The queen made another proposal, and commanded them to show on what principle they neglected to take the sacraments of the body and blood of Christ on the holy day of Easter, according to the custom of the holy and apostolic church. They replied, saying: "The apostle, speaking of this, says: 'He that eats and drinks unworthily, eats and drinks judgement upon himself.' Therefore because we recognize that we are sinners, we dread to approach that mystery, lest we eat and drink judgement upon ourselves."

The queen said to them: "Why then, shall all who are sinners not taste the sacred mystery? In that case, none ought to take it; because none is without stain of sin, not even the babe whose life is but one day upon the earth. And if none ought to partake of it, why does the gospel proclaim in the Lord's words: 'Unless you eat the flesh of the son of man, and drink his blood, you shall not have life within you'? But it is clearly necessary that you should otherwise understand the sentence that you quote from the apostle, in accordance with the understanding of the fathers; for he does not judge that all sinners take the sacraments of salvation unworthily: when he had said, 'eats and drinks judgement upon himself,' he added, 'eats and drinks judgement on himself, if he discern not the Lord's body': that is, if he does not distinguish it in faith from physical foods. He also who presumes to approach the sacred mysteries without confession and repentance, in the filth of his crimes, he, I say, eats and drinks judgement upon himself. But we, who many days before have made confession of sins, and are scourged with penitence, and made lean with fasting; and are cleansed from the pollution of sin by alms and tears: we approach the Lord's table in catholic faith on the day of the Lord's resurrection, and we take the flesh and blood of the spotless lamb, Jesus Christ, not for judgement, but for remission of sins; and in salutary preparation for participation in eternal bliss."

Hearing these things from her, they could answer nothing; and they recognised thenceforth the church's statutes, and kept them in participating in the salutary mystery.

Moreover there were some, in certain districts of the Scots, who were wont to celebrate mass contrary to the custom of the whole church; with I know not what barbarous rite. This the queen, fired with the zeal for God, so sought to destroy and uproot, that thenceforward none appeared in the whole Scottish nation who dared do such a thing.

They were accustomed also to neglect reverence for the Lord's days; and thus to continue upon them as upon other days all the labours of earthly work. But she showed, both by reason and by authority, that this was not permitted. She said: "Let us hold the Lord's day in veneration because of the Lord's resurrection, which took place upon it; and let us not do servile labours upon [the day] in which we know that we were redeemed from the devil's servitude. This too the blessed pope Gregory affirms, saying: 'On Sundays we must cease earthly labour, and apply ourselves only to prayers; so that whatever negligence has occurred during the six days may be expiated with prayers during the day of the Lord's resurrection.' The same father Gregory also punished a certain man with severe rebuke, because of earthly labour that he had done on the Lord's day; and passed decree of excommunication for two months upon those by whose counsels he had done it."

They were unable to oppose these arguments of the wise queen: and at her instigation so preserved reverence for the Lord's days thereafter, that none dared on those days to carry any burdens, or to compel another to do so.

Illegal wedlock with step-mothers, as also a surviving brother's marriage with the wife of a brother who had died, (unions that used to take place there previously) she showed to be exceedingly execrable, and to be avoided by the faithful like death itself. Many other things too, which had sprung up contrary to the rule of faith and the statutes of ecclesiastical observances, she took pains to condemn in the same council, and to cast out from within the boundaries of her kingdom. All the measures that she had proposed she so supported by the testimony of scripture, and by declarations of the holy fathers, that [the Scots] were unable to reply with anything at all in opposition to them; but on the contrary they laid aside their obstinacy and agreed to reason, and gladly received them all for fulfilment.

Chapter 9: How greatly she was given to compunction and to prayer, also the works of fasting and of mercy.

The venerable queen who had exerted herself to cleanse the house of God, God helping her, from pollutions and errors, merited herself to become from day to day a worthy temple of God, the holy Spirit illuminating her heart. That she was this in truth, I know extremely well; because I have both seen her external works, and have known her conscience, by her own revealing. For she deigned to speak to me most intimately, and to expose her secret thoughts; not because there was anything good in me, but because she thought that there was. When she spoke to me of the salvation of the soul, and of the sweetness of eternal life, she uttered words full of all grace, words that truly were spoken with her mouth by the holy Spirit, dwelling in her heart. And in speaking she was so moved that you would have thought her all dissolved in tears; so that by her emotion my mind was moved to weeping. More than all the people I have yet known, she was devoted to the practices of prayer and fasting, and to works of mercy and of alms.

To speak first of her praying, none present in the church was more silent, but none was more intent in prayer. It was her custom never to speak of anything secular in the house of God, to conduct no affair of earth, but only to pray; and praying to shed tears, in her body alone upon earth, but in mind close to God: for her pure prayer sought nothing but God, and the things that were God's. But what shall I say of her fasting; except that by excessive abstinence she brought on the molestation of a very serious disease?

With these two practices, of prayer and abstinence, she united the good works of mercy. What was gentler than her bosom? Who kinder to the needy? She would gladly have given not only her substance, but herself also, if it had been permissible, to a poor person. She was poorer herself than all her poor: for they had not, but desired to have; while she took pains to scatter what she had. When she walked or rode in public, crowds of wretched men, of orphans, of widows, flocked to her as to a kindest mother; and of these none departed from her without consolation. And when she had distributed everything that she had carried about with her for the benefit of the needy, she used to take as gifts for the poor clothing or any other things that those who were with her, whether rich men or attendants, had at the time; so that a poor man should never go sorrowful away. Those with her did not take it ill, but on the contrary competed to offer her their belongings; since they knew certainly that they would all be restored to them twice over by her. Occasionally also she took something that belonged to the king, no matter what, to give to a destitute man; a pious robbery, which he always took altogether willingly and gladly. Seeing that he was accustomed to offer at [Christ's] Mandate on the Lord's Supper,[5] and at the celebrations of mass, [specially minted] golden coins, from these she used very often to steal some piously, and to bestow them upon a poor man who had importuned her. And indeed often when the king knew of it, he pretended not to know, because he delighted very much in such theft; and sometimes he seized her hand with the coins, and brought her to me for judgement, saying in jest that she was a thief.

With cheerfulness of heart she showed the munificence of her generosity not to the native poor alone, but also to poor of almost all nations, when they hastened to the renown of her compassion. One may say of her indeed: "She has scattered, she has given to the poor: therefore her justice remains for ever and ever."

And who can tell in number how many men, and how great, she restored to liberty, by payment of a price; men whom the ferocity of their enemies had led away captive from the nation of the Angles, and reduced to slavery? She had even sent secret spies everywhere throughout the provinces of the Scots, to find out which of the captives were oppressed with the harshest servitude, and treated most inhumanly; and to report to her minutely the place where and the people by whom they were oppressed: and she had compassion upon such [slaves] from her inmost heart, and hastened quickly to help them, to ransom them, and restore them to liberty.

At that time very many men, shut up in cells apart, in various places in the districts of the Scots, were living in the flesh, but not according to the flesh; for they led the life of angels upon earth. The queen endeavoured to venerate and love Christ in them; and to visit them very often with her presence and conversation, and to commend herself to their prayers. And when she could not persuade them to agree to accept from her anything, she humbly begged them to deign to enjoin upon her some act of charity or mercy. And without delay she fulfilled devoutly whatever was their will; either in delivering the poor from penury, or in relieving the afflicted of the miseries by which they were distressed.

And since the church of St Andrews is frequented by the religious devotion of visitors from the peoples round about, she had built dwellings upon either shore of the sea that separates Lothian and Scotland; so that pilgrims and poor might turn aside there to rest, after the labour of the journey; and might find there ready everything that necessity might require for the restoration of the body. She appointed attendants for this purpose alone, to have always ready all that was needed for guests, and to wait upon them with great care. She provided for them also ships, to carry them across, both going and returning, without ever demanding any price for the passage from those who were to be taken over.

Chapter 10: How she used to act before the Lord's Nativity, and in Lent.
I have described the daily life of the venerable queen, and have also said something of her daily works of mercy; now I shall attempt to tell briefly how she was accustomed to pass the forty days before the Lord's Nativity, and the whole time of Lent.

After resting for a short time in the beginning of the night, she entered the church, and she alone completed the matins first of the holy Trinity, then of the holy Cross, afterwards of St Mary; and after finishing these she began the offices for the dead. After this she began the psalter, and ceased not till she had gone through it to the end. At the proper hour priests celebrated morning Lauds; and meanwhile she either concluded the psalter which she had begun, or if she had finished it once she began it a second time. And when the service of morning Lauds was ended, she used to return to her chamber; and with the king himself to wash the feet of six poor persons, and to give them something to ease their poverty. It was indeed the chamberlain's chief care to bring in the poor each night before the entrance of the queen, so that when she came in to serve them she should find them ready.

All this concluded, she betook herself to rest and sleep.

After rising from bed in the early morning, she continued long in prayers and psalms; and between the chants she performed a work of mercy. She caused to be brought in to her in the first hour of the day nine baby orphans, destitute of all support: she had ordered the softer foods, in which the age of babyhood delights, to be prepared for them each day; and when they were brought she deigned to place them on her knees; to make their little drinks for them, and to put food into their mouths with the spoons that she used herself. Thus the queen who was honoured by the whole population filled for Christ's sake the part of a servant and a kindest mother. She might very properly have used the words of the blessed Job: "Compassion grew up with me from my infancy, and left with me my mother's womb."

The custom was to bring in meanwhile, into the royal palace, three hundred poor. These were seated around in order; and when the king and queen had entered, the servants closed the doors: because (excepting certain religious chaplains, and other attendants) none was permitted to be present at their works of charity. The king taking the one side, the queen taking the other, they served Christ in the poor; and with great devotion offered them food and drink specially prepared for the purpose.

This done, the queen would enter the church; and there with protracted prayers and tearful groanings would offer herself as a sacrifice to God. On these holy days, within the space of night and day (in addition to the services of holy Trinity, of holy Cross, and of St Mary) she completed two repetitions of the psalter, or three: and before the celebration of public mass she had five or six masses performed before her privately.

These things completed, when the time of dining approached, she (humbly serving) refreshed twenty-four poor persons before taking her own refection. For in addition to all the charities of which I have told above, she supported, the whole year round, as long as she lived, poor people to that number—that is, of twenty-four. She had arranged that these should stay with her wherever she dwelt, and accompany her wherever she went.

And after she had devoutly served Christ in them, she used to refresh her own little body also. But because she did not (as the apostle says) "make provision for the flesh, in its desires," she had in this refection barely enough to satisfy the necessities of life. She ate merely in order to preserve life, not to yield to pleasure. The light and moderate repast provoked hunger instead of satisfying it. She seemed to taste food rather than to consume it. Gather from this, I ask you, the extent and manner of her continence in fasting, when such was her abstinence in feasting.

And although she passed her whole life in great continence, yet in these days, the forty before Easter and the forty before Christmas, she used to afflict herself with incredible abstinence. Because of the excessive rigour of her fasting, she suffered acutest pain in her stomach to the end of her days; yet the infirmity of her body did not diminish her virtue in good works: she remained studious in sacred reading, persistent in prayer; never failing in charities, wholly employed with vigilance in all things that were God's. And because she knew that it is written, "Whom the Lord loves he reproves; and he scourges every son whom he receives," she gladly accepted with patience and rendering of thanks her bodily suffering, as the scourging of her gentlest Father.

Chapter 11: How the Lord showed something in witness of her holy life.

Thus given up to these works, and others like them; and labouring under constant infirmities, so that according to the apostle's words "virtue was perfected in infirmity": she rose from virtue to virtue, and became better from day to day. Abandoning in her mind all earthly things, she burned with full desire in her thirst for heavenly things; and said with the psalmist, crying aloud with heart and mouth, "My heart has thirsted for God, the living spring: when shall I come, and appear before God's face?"

Let others admire in others the signs of miracles; I esteem much more in Margaret the works of mercy. Signs are common to the good and to the bad; but works of true piety and love are peculiar to the good. The former sometimes show sanctity; the latter constitute sanctity. Let us, I repeat, more worthily admire in Margaret the deeds that made her holy, than the miracles, if she had done any; since they could only show her holiness to men. Let us more worthily hold her in awe, because through her devotion to justice, piety, mercy, and love, we contemplate in her, rather than miracles, the deeds of the ancient fathers.

Yet I shall relate an occurrence which I think it pertinent to tell, as regarding the evidence of her religious life.

She had had a book of gospels, adorned with jewels and gold; and in it the figures of the four evangelists were decorated with painting, interspersed with gold: and also every capital letter glowed all in gold. This volume she had always cherished very dearly, beyond the others in which she had been accustomed to read and study. This volume she was carrying, when she chanced to be crossing over a ford; and the book, being not carefully enough wrapped up in cloths, fell into the middle of the water. The carrier, not knowing this, concluded unconcernedly the journey that he had begun: and he first learned what he had lost, when he wished afterwards to produce the book. It was long sought without being found. At last it was found lying open in the bottom of the river, its leaves being constantly kept in motion by the current of the water; and the little sheets of silk that had covered the golden letters to prevent their being dimmed by contact with the leaves, had been torn out by the rapidity of the river. Who would have thought the book worth anything any longer? Who would have believed that even one letter in it would have remained visible? But indeed it was drawn out from the middle of the river entire, undecayed, unhurt, so that it appeared not to have been touched by the water at all. The whiteness of the leaves, and the unimpaired beauty of the letters throughout, remained as they had been before it had fallen into the river; except that in parts of the last leaves some mark of moisture could just be seen. The book was brought back and the miracle related to the queen; and she returned thanks to Christ, and cherished the volume much more dearly than before. So let others see what they think of it; I hold that this sign was given by the Lord, because of his love for the venerable queen.

Chapter 12: How she foreknew her death, and foretold certain things in the future.

Meanwhile, when already almighty God was preparing to render the eternal rewards of her pious labours, she made herself ready for the entrance into the other life much more sedulously than had been her wont. For, as will presently be shown from her own words, she seemed to have long foreknown her departure from this life, and other future events. She therefore spoke to me privately, and began to relate her life to me in order; and to pour out rivers of tears at every word. So great indeed was her remorse in the conversation, so great a torrent of weeping had sprung from her remorse, that there was certainly nothing, so it seemed to me, that she could not at that time have obtained from Christ. While she wept, I wept also; weeping long, we were meanwhile silent; because we could utter no words, for the rising sobs. The flame of remorse which had burned up her heart had touched my mind also through her spiritual words. And while I listened to the words of the holy Spirit spoken with her tongue, and gazed through her words upon her conscience, I counted myself unworthy of so great favour of her friendship.

When she had finished speaking of necessities, she began again to speak to me thus. "Farewell" she said, "I shall not continue much longer in this life; and thou wilt live a long time after me. There are two things that I request of thee: one, that thou remember my soul in thy masses and prayers all thy life; the other, that thou take charge of my sons and daughters, and afford them love; and especially teach them, and never cease to teach them, to fear and love God. And when thou seest any one of them elevated to the zenith of earthly dignity, that thou be to him especially a father and instructor; exhorting him, and when circumstances require it reproving him, to the end that he be not inflated with pride by reason of his temporary honour; that he offend not God by avarice; that through prosperity in this world he neglect not the felicity of eternal life. This" she said, "is what I ask thee, before God, who is the third here present with us, to promise me carefully to perform."

Again bursting into tears at these words, I promised diligently to do what she had asked; for I dared not gainsay her, whom I had heard thus unhesitatingly foretell the future. The event proves that things are now as she foretold; because I both live after her death, and see her offspring raised to the rank of honour.

Having ended our conference, returning home I bade the queen farewell for the last time; for I never saw her again.

Chapter 13: How she departed from this life.

Not long afterwards she was attacked by more violent illness than she had before; and before the day of her summons she was wasted by the fire of a long disease.

I shall relate her death, as I have heard it from her priest. She had loved him more intimately than the rest, because of his simplicity, innocence, and chastity; and after the queen's death he gave himself up to the perpetual service of Christ for the sake of her soul, and offered himself as a sacrifice for her at the tomb of the incorrupt body of the most blessed father Cuthbert. He was inseparably present in the last hours of the queen's life, and he had commended her soul to Christ with prayers as it passed from her body. As he had watched her departure throughout, and since I often question him about it, he is accustomed to relate it thus, with tears:

"For half a year" he says, "and somewhat more, she was never able to sit on horseback; and seldom to rise from bed. On the fourth day before her death, while the king was upon an expedition, and she could not have known from the swiftness of any messenger what was happening to him on that day, at so great distance away over the land, she became suddenly sadder, and said this to us who sat beside her: 'Perhaps today so great an evil has happened to the kingdom of the Scots, as has not happened for many ages past.'

"When we heard this, we received her words with little attention at the time; but after some days a messenger arrived, and we learned that the king had been killed on the same day upon which the queen had thus spoken. As if foreseeing the future, she had strongly opposed his going with any army; but it happened, I know not for what reason, that on this occasion he did not obey her warnings.

"When the fourth day after the slaying of the king arrived, her infirmity being somewhat lightened, she entered the oratory, to hear mass; and there she took care to prepare for her death, which was already imminent, with the sacred *viaticum* of the body and blood of the Lord. After having been revived by the salutary gust of these, she was presently troubled with a return of her former pains; and was prostrated in bed: and, as the malady increased, she was driven violently on towards her death.

"But [you ask] what I am doing; why I delay? I fear to come to her decease, just as if I could postpone longer the death of my lady, and prolong her life. But all flesh is grass, and all its glory is as the flower of grass; the grass has withered, and the flower has fallen.

"Her face had already paled in death when she bade me, and the other attendants of the sacred altar along with me, to stand beside her, and to commend her soul to Christ with song. She also commanded to bring her the cross that she used to call the Black Cross, and which she used always to hold in the greatest veneration. And when the shrine in which it had been enclosed could not be opened very quickly, the queen groaned heavily, and said: 'Oh wretch that we are, and guilty! We shall not be judged worthy to see again the Holy Rood!' When, however, it was brought out of the case, and taken to her, she received it with reverence; and set to embracing and kissing it, and signing with it very frequently her eyes and face.

"And now her whole body grew cold, although warmth still pulsed in her breast; but none the less she prayed continually. Singing the fiftieth psalm[6] right through, she held the cross before her eyes the while, grasping it with both hands.

"Meanwhile her son, who still at present holds the government after his father, returned from the army, and entered the queen's bedchamber. What distress had he then; what agony of mind! He stood there, harassed by misfortunes on all sides; he knew not whither to turn. For he had come to announce to his mother that his father and his brother had been slain; and he found that his mother, whom he had loved especially, was just on the brink of death: whom first to mourn, he knew not. But the departure of his sweetest mother, whom he saw lying almost dead before his eyes, tore his heart with the sharpest pangs. In addition to all this, anxiety for the state of the kingdom weighed upon him; because he knew with certainty that it would be disturbed by his father's death. On all sides grief, on all sides pain, had entangled him.

"While the queen, lying as in an agony, was thought by those present to be dead, she suddenly rallied her strength and addressed her son. She questioned him about his father and brother; but he would not tell her the truth, lest hearing of their death she too should instantly die: so he answered that they were well. But she sighed deeply, and said, 'I know, my son, I know. I adjure thee by this holy cross, by the nearness of our relationship, to speak out what thou knowest to be true.' He was compelled to disclose the matter as it had occurred.

"What shouldst thou have thought she would have done—who would not have believed that she would have murmured against God, in so many adversities? At the same time she had lost her husband, she had lost a son, disease had tortured her to death: but in all this she sinned not with her lips; she spoke no foolish word against God. Instead, she raised her eyes and her hands to heaven, and broke into praise and thanksgiving, saying: 'I render praises and thanks to thee, almighty God, who hast willed that I should endure such anguish at my death; and to cleanse me, as I hope, by enduring it, from some stains of sin.'

"She had perceived that death was there; and immediately she began a prayer, which is said by the priest after tasting the Lord's body and blood, thus: 'Lord Jesus Christ, who by the Father's will, with the co-operation of the holy Spirit, hast given the world life through death, deliver me.' While she was saying 'deliver me,' her soul was released from the chains of the body, and departed to Christ, whom she had always loved, the author of true liberty; becoming a sharer in the felicity of those whose example of virtue she had followed. Her departure took place with so great calm, with so complete tranquillity, that it is not to be doubted that her soul departed to the region of eternal rest and peace. And strangely her face, which had become all pallid in death, as is usual in the dying, was so suffused after her death with red upon white that she might have been believed to be not dead, but sleeping.

"So we enshrouded her body honourably, as befitted a queen; and carried it to the church of Holy Trinity, which she herself had built; and gave her burial in it, as she had commanded, opposite the altar and the venerable symbol of the holy cross, which she herself had erected there. And thus her body now rests in the place where she used to afflict it with vigils and prayers, with shedding of tears and bowing of knees."[7]

St Margaret's family connections. ▶

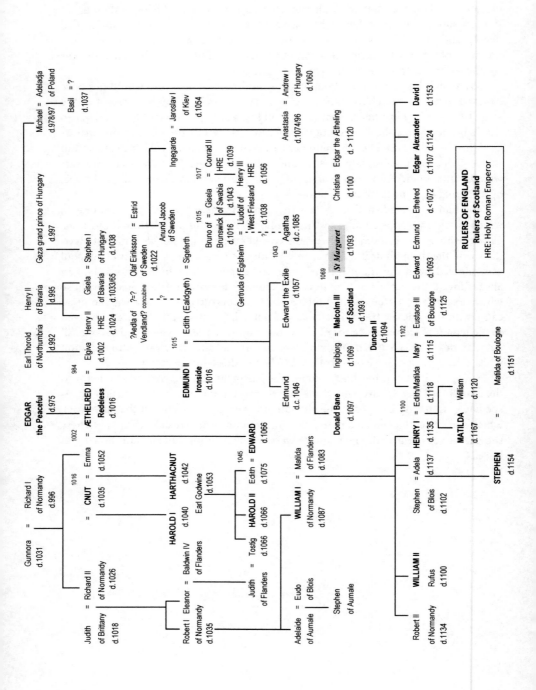

RULERS OF ENGLAND
Rulers of Scotland
HRE: Holy Roman Emperor

Bibliography

** indicates that this edition was accessible on the Internet
Archive (www.archive.org) at the time of publication.*

Adam of Bremen	Adam of Bremen, *Gesta Hammaburgensis Ecclesiae Pontificum* [c.1080]: G. Waitz, *Adami Gesta Hammaburgensis Ecclesiae Pontificum ex recensione Lappenbergh* (Scriptores rerum Germanicarum, 2nd edn 1876*)
Aelred, *Edward*	Aelred of Rievaulx, *The Life of Saint Edward, King and Confessor* [c.1163]: Freeland & Dutton, pp. 123–243
Aelred, *Genealogy*	Aelred of Rievaulx, *The Genealogy of the Kings of the English* [c.1154]: Freeland & Dutton, pp. 71–122
Aelred, *Lament*	Aelred of Rievaulx, *Lament for David, King of the Scots* [c.1154]: Freeland & Dutton, pp. 45–70
Aird, *Miracles*	W. M. Aird, "The Making of a Medieval Miracle Collection: The *Liber de translationibus et miraculis Sancti Cuthberti*", in *Northern History* 28 (1992), pp. 1–24
Aird, *William of St Calais*	W. M. Aird, "An Absent Friend: The Career of Bishop William of St Calais", in Rollason, Harvey & Prestwich, pp. 283–297
Anderson, *Annals*	Alan O. Anderson (tr.), *Scottish Annals from English Chronicles 500–1256* (Nutt, 1908*)
Anderson I & II	Alan Orr Anderson (tr.), *Early Sources of Scottish History* I & II (Oliver and Boyd, 1922*)
Anselm	*Sancti Anselmi cantuariensis archiepiscopi Opera Omnia* [d.1109]: F. S. Schmitt (ed.), *Sancti Anselmi cantuariensis archiepiscopi opera omnia* I–VI (1938–1961)
Arnold I & II	Thomas Arnold (ed.), *Symeonis monachi opera omnia* I (Rolls Series 75, 1882), II (Rolls Series 75, 1885)
ASC	*Anglo-Saxon Chronicle*: Anne Savage (tr.), *The Anglo-Saxon Chronicles* (Phoebe Phillips/Heinemann, 1982)
Atkinson	J. C. Atkinson (ed.), *Cartularium abbathiae de Whiteby, Ordinis S. Benedicti: fundatae anno MLXXVIII* (Surtees Society 69, 1878*)
Baker	Malcolm Baker, "Medieval Illustrations of Bede's Life of Cuthbert", in *Journal of the Warburg and Courtauld Institutes* 41 (1978), pp. 16–49
Barrow, *Kingdom*	G. W. S. Barrow, *The Kingdom of the Scots* (Arnold 1973, Edinburgh University Press, 2003)
Barrow, *Kings*	G. W. S. Barrow, "The Kings of Scotland and Durham", in Rollason, Harvey & Prestwich, pp. 311–323

Bartlett	R. J. Bartlett (ed.), *History and Historians: Selected Papers of R. W. Southern* (Wiley-Blackwell, 2004)
Battiscombe	C. F. Battiscombe (ed.), *The Relics of Saint Cuthbert* (Oxford University Press, 1956)
Bede, *HE*	Bede, *Historia ecclesiastica gentis Anglorum* [731]: Leo Sherley-Price (tr.), rev. L. E. Latham, *A History of the English Church and People* (Penguin, 1955 rev. 1968)
Bede, *Vita*	Bede, *Vita sancti Cuthberti prosaica auctore Beda* [c.721]: J. F. Webb (tr.), "Bede: Life of Cuthbert" in D. H. Farmer (ed.), *The Age of Bede* (Penguin, 1965 rev. 1983)
Bethell	Denis Bethell, "Two Letters of Pope Paschal II to Scotland", in *Scottish Historical Review* 49 (1970), pp. 33–45
Billings	Robert William Billings, *Architectural Illustrations and Description of the Cathedral Church at Durham* (Boone, 1843*, Nabu Press facsimile reprint on demand)
Bilson, *Chronology*	John Bilson, "Durham Cathedral: the Chronology of its Vaults", in *Archaeological Journal* 79 (1922), pp. 101–60
Bilson, *Discoveries*	John Bilson, "Recent Discoveries at the East End of the Cathedral Church of Durham", in *Archaeological Journal* 53 (1896*), pp. 1–18
Bilson, *Vaulting*	John Bilson, "The Beginnings of Gothic Architecture II: Norman Vaulting in England", in *Journal of the Royal Institute of British Architects* 6 (1899), pp. 25–326
Blunt	J. Blunt, "St Cuthbert and his Patrimony", in *Journal of the British Archaeological Association* 22 (1866*), pp. 420–42
Bony, *French Gothic*	Jean Bony, *French Gothic Architecture of the Twelfth and Thirteenth Centuries* (University of California, 1983)
Bony, *Stonework*	Jean Bony, "The Stonework Planning of the First Durham Master", in Eric Fernie & Paul Crossley (eds.), *Medieval Architecture and its Intellectual Context: Studies in Honour of Peter Kidson* (Hambledon Press, 1990), pp. 19–34
Borg	Alan Borg, "The Development of Chevron Ornament", in *Journal of the British Archaeological Association* 30 (1967)
Botfield	B. Botfield, *Catalogi veteres librorum ecclesiae cathedralis Dunelmensis* (Surtees Society 7, 1838*)
Briggs, Cambridge & Bailey	H. Denis Briggs, Eric Cambridge & Richard N. Bailey, "A New Approach to Church Archaeology", in *Archaeologia Aeliana* 5th ser. 11 (1983), pp. 91–7
Cambridge	Eric Cambridge, "Why did the Community of St Cuthbert Settle in Chester-le-Street?", in Gerald Bonner, David Rollason & Clare Stancliffe (eds.), *St*

	Cuthbert, His Cult and His Community to AD 1200 (Boydell Press, 1989), pp. 367–386
Chambre	William de Chambre, *Continuatio historiae Dunelmensis* [*c.*1365]: Raine, *Scriptores*, pp. 125–156
Chaplais	Pierre Chaplais, "William of Saint-Calais and the Domesday Survey", in J. C. Holt (ed.), *Domesday Studies* (Boydell Press, 1987), pp. 65–78
Clapham	A. W. Clapham, *English Romanesque Architecture after the Conquest* I & II (Clarendon Press, 1934)
Clark	John Willis Clark (ed. and tr.), *The Observances in Use at the Augustinian Priory of S. Giles and S. Andrew at Barnwell, Cambridgeshire* [13th century] (Macmillan and Bowes, 1897*)
Clover & Gibson	Helen Clover & Margaret Gibson (eds. and trs.), *The Letters of Lanfranc, Archbishop of Canterbury* [d.1089] (Clarendon Press, 1979)
Coldingham	Geoffrey de Coldingham, *De statu ecclesiae Dunelmensis* [*c.*1214]: Raine, *Scriptores*, pp. 3–31
Coldstream & Draper	Nicola Coldstream and Peter Draper (eds.), *Medieval Art and Architecture at Durham Cathedral* (British Archaeological Association Transactions 3, 1980)
Colgrave	B. Colgrave, "The Post-Bedan Translations and Miracles of St Cuthbert", in Cyril Fox & Bruce Dickins (eds.), *The Early Cultures of North-west Europe* (Cambridge University Press, 1950), pp. 306–332
Craster E	E. Craster, "The Patrimony of St Cuthbert", in *English Historical Review* 69 (1954) pp. 177–199
Craster H	H. H. E. Craster, "A Contemporary Record of the Pontificate of Ranulf Flambard", in *Archaeologia Aeliana* 4th series 7 (1930) No. XIX, pp. 33–56
Crook	John Crook, "The Architectural Setting of the Cult of St Cuthbert in Durham Cathedral (1093–1200)", in Rollason, Harvey & Prestwich, pp. 235–250
David	C. W. David, "A Tract attributed to Simeon of Durham", in *English Historical Review* 32 (1917*), pp. 382–7
Davis	H. W. C. Davis (ed.), *Regesta regum Anglo-Normannorum* I (Clarendon Press, 1913*)
DB	*Domesday Book*: Ann Williams & G. H. Martin (eds.), *Domesday Book: A Complete Translation* (Alecto, 1992, Penguin, 2002)
De miraculis	*Liber de miraculis et translationibus Sancti Cuthberti* [*c.*1123]: Arnold I, pp. 229–61, Arnold II, pp. 333–362; (cf. *HTC*: Hinde, pp. 158–201); translation by R. A. B. Mynors in Battiscombe, pp. 99–107, based on Raine, *Cuthbert*, pp. 74–85
Delisle	Leopold Delisle (ed.), *Rouleaux des morts du ixe au xve siècle* (Paris, 1866*)

Devonshire & Wilkie	C. Devonshire & R. Wilkie, "The Building of the Cathedral", in Jackson, pp. 16–31
DIV	*De iniusta vexacione Willelmi episcopi*: Arnold I, pp. 170–95, Stevenson, pp. 731–750, Offler, *DIV*, pp. 321–341
Douglas	David C. Douglas, *William the Conqueror* (University of California Press, 1964)
Dowden	John Dowden, *The Bishops of Scotland*, ed. J. Maitland Thomson (MacLehose, 1912*)
Durham Obitals	MS Durham Cathedral B.4.24 and British Library MS Harley 1804 13: transcribed in J. Stevenson (ed.), *Liber Vitae Ecclesie Dunelmensis nec non obituaria duo ejusdem ecclesiie* (London, 1841*), pp. 135–148 and 149–152.
Eadmer	Eadmer, *Historia novorum in Anglia* [*c*.1122]: Martin Rule (ed.), *Eadmer historia novorum in Anglia* (Rolls Series 81, 1884*)
Farrer	William Farrer, *An Outline Itinerary of King Henry the First* (reprinted from *English Historical Review* 34, 1919, pp. 303–381, 505*)
Fernie	Eric Fernie, *The Architecture of Norman England* (Oxford University Press, 2000)
Ferrey	Benjamin Ferrey, "Some Remarks on Points of Resemblance, &c., between the Naves of Christchurch and Durham", in *Gentleman's Magazine* NS 40 (211) (1861*), pp. 607–10
Fleming, Honour & Pevsner	John Fleming, Hugh Honour & Nikolaus Pevsner, *The Penguin Dictionary of Architecture and Landscape Architecture* (Penguin, 5th edn. 1988)
Florence	Florence of Worcester, *Monachi chronicon ex chronicis* [*c*.1140]: Benjamin Thorpe (ed.), *Florenti Wigorniensis monachi chronicon ex chronicis* II (English Historical Society, 1849*,1880); Joseph Stevenson (tr.), "The Chronicle of Florence of Worcester", in *The Church Historians of England* II i (Seeleys 1853*), pp. 169–404
Fordun	John of Fordun, *Chronica Gentis Scotorum* [*c*.1380]: William F. Skene (ed.), *Johannis de Fordun Chronica Gentis Scotorum* (The Historians of Scotland I); translation Felix J. H. Skene, *John of Fordun's Chronicle of the Scottish Nation* (The Historians of Scotland IV) (Edmonston and Douglas, 1871* and 1872*)
Forster	R. H. Forster, "Turgot, Prior of Durham", in *Journal of the British Archaeological Association* 13 (1907*), pp. 32–40
Fowler, *Accounts*	J. T. Fowler (ed.), *Extracts from the Account Rolls of the Abbey of Durham* II (Surtees Society 100, 1899*)

Fowler, *Excavations*   J. T. Fowler, "An Account of the Excavations made on the Site of the Chapterhouse of Durham Cathedral in 1874", in *Archaeologia* 45/2 (1880*), pp. 385–404

Fowler, *Rites*   J. T. Fowler (ed.), *Rites of Durham* [16th century] (Surtees Society 107, 1902*)

Freeland & Dutton   Jane Patricia Freeland (tr.) & Marsha L. Dutton (ed.), *Aelred of Rievaulx: the Historical Works* (Cistercian Publications, 2005)

Freeman   Edward A. Freeman, *The History of the Norman Conquest: Its Causes and its Results* II (Clarendon Press, 1868*)

Gaimar   Geoffroi Gaimar, *L'Estoire des Engleis* [12th century]: Joseph Stevenson (tr.), "Gaimar", in *The Church Historians of England* II ii (Seeleys, 1854*), pp. 729–810

Galbraith   V. H. Galbraith, *Domesday Book: Its Place in Administrative History* (Clarendon Press, 1974)

Gee   Eric Gee, "Discoveries in the Frater at Durham", in *Archaeological Journal* 123 (1966), pp. 69–78

Gem   Richard Gem, *Studies in English Pre-Romanesque and Romanesque Architecture* I & II (Pindar Press, 2003)

Gem & Thurlby   Richard Gem & Malcolm Thurlby, "The Early Monastic Church at Lastingham", in Lawrence R. Hoey (ed.), *Yorkshire Monasticism, Archaeology, Art and Architecture* (British Archaeological Association Transactions 15, 1995), pp. 31–9

Graystanes   Robert de Graystanes, *Historia de statu ecclesiae Dunelmensis* [c.1333]: Raine, *Scriptores*, pp. 33–123

Green   Lionel Green, *Daughter Houses of Merton Priory* (Merton Historical Society, 2002)

Greenwell, *Cathedral*   William Greenwell, *Durham Cathedral* (Andrews 1879, 1889*, 1904)

Greenwell, *Drawings*   W. Greenwell, "Drawings of Parts of the Cathedral, Durham, Made at the End of the Eighteenth Century", in *Transactions of the Architectural and Archaeological Society of Durham and Northumberland* 5, 1896–1905 (1907), pp. 29–36 & plates following

Greenwell, *Feodarium*   W. Greenwell (ed.), *Feodarium Prioratus Dunelmensis. A survey of the estates of the prior and convent of Durham compiled in the fifteenth century* (Surtees Society 58, 1872*)

Gullick   Michael Gullick, "The Scribes of the Durham Cantor's book (Durham, Dean and Chapter Library B.IV.24) and the Durham Martyrology Scribe", in Rollason, Harvey & Prestwich, pp. 93–124

Haddan & Stubbs   Arthur West Haddan & William Stubbs, *Councils and Ecclesiastical Documents Relating to Great Britain and Ireland* II i (Clarendon Press, 1873*)

Harrison	Julian Harrison, "The Mortuary Roll of Turgot of Durham (d.1115)", in *Scriptorium* 58 (2004), pp. 67–83
Hegge	Robert Hegge, *The Legend of St Cuthbert* [1626]: John Brough Taylor (ed.) (Garbutt, 1816*)
Hills	Gordon M. Hills, "The Cathedral and Monastery of St Cuthbert at Durham", in *Journal of the British Archaeological Association* 22 (1866*), pp. 197–237
Hinde	J. Hodgson Hinde (ed.), *Symeonis Dunelmensis opera et Collectanea* I (Surtees Society 51, 1868*)
Hohler	C. Hohler, "The Cathedral of St Swithun at Stavanger in the Twelfth Century", in *Journal of the British Archaeological Association* 27 (1964), pp. 92–118
Hope	W. H. St. John Hope, "Notes on Recent Excavations in the Cloister of Durham Abbey", in *Proceedings of the Society of Antiquaries* 2nd ser. 22 (1909), pp. 416–424
Hope & Fowler	W. H. St. John Hope & J. T. Fowler, "Recent Discoveries in the Cloister of Durham Abbey, with Introduction by Canon J. T. Fowler", in *Archaeologia* 58 (1903), pp. 437–460
Hoveden	Roger of Hoveden, *Cronica* [c.1201]: William Stubbs (ed.), *Chronica magistri Rogeri de Hovedene* I (Rolls Series 51, 1868); Henry T. Riley (tr.), *The Annals of Roger of Hoveden* I (Bohn, 1853*)
HSC	*Historia de Sancto Cuthberto* [c.1050]: Arnold I, pp. 196–214
HTC	*Historia translationem Sancti Cuthberti* [c.1123]: Hinde, pp. 158–201; (cf. *De miraculis*: Arnold I, pp. 229–61, Arnold II, pp. 333–362)
Hugh the Chanter	Hugh the Chanter, *The History of the Church of York 1066–1127* [d.1140]: Charles Johnson (ed. and tr.), *Hugh the Chanter: The History of the Church of York 1066–1127* (Clarendon Press, 1990)
Huneycutt	Lois L. Huneycutt, *Matilda of Scotland: A Study in Medieval Queenship* (Boydell Press, 2003)
Hutchinson I & II	William Hutchinson, *The History & Antiquities of the County Palatine of Durham* I (Newcastle, 1786, Durham, 1823*), II (Newcastle, 1787*)
Jackson	Michael Jackson (ed.), *Engineering a Cathedral* (Telford, 1993)
James	John James, "The Rib Vaults of Durham Cathedral", in *Gesta* 22/2 (1983), pp. 135–145
Johnson	G. A. L. Johnson, "The Geological Setting of Durham Cathedral", in Jackson, pp. 109–119
Johnson & Cronne	Charles Johnson & H. A. Cronne (ed.), *Regesta regum Anglo-Normannorum* II (Clarendon Press, 1956*)
Kjølbye-Biddle	Birthe Kjølbye-Biddle, "The 7th Century Minster at Winchester interpreted", in L. A. S. Butler & R. K.

Morris (eds.), *The Anglo-Saxon Church: Papers on History, Architecture and Archaeology in Honour of Dr H. M. Taylor* (CBA Research Report 60, 1986*) pp. 196-209

Knowles — David Knowles, *The Monastic Order in England 940-1216* (Cambridge University Press, 2nd edn. 1963)

Lang — Andrew Lang, *St Andrews* (Longmans, Green, 1893*)

Lawrie — Archibald C. Lawrie (ed.) *Early Scottish Charters prior to AD 1153* (MacLehose, 1905*)

LDE Cont — Symeon of Durham, *LDE Continuation*: Arnold I, pp. 135-69, Rollason, *LDE*, pp. 266/7-322/3, Stevenson, pp. 712-730

le Neve — John le Neve, *Fasti Ebor*: Diana E. Greenway (ed.), *John le Neve fasti Ecclesiae Anglicanae 1066-1300 VI: York* (Institute of Historical Research, 1968)

Liber Vitae — David & Lynda Rollason (eds.), *The Durham Liber Vitae: London, British Library, MS Cotton Domitian A.VII: edition and digital facsimile with introduction, codicological, prosopographical and linguistic commentary, and indexes; including the Biographical register of Durham Cathedral Priory (1083-1539) by A. J. Piper*, 3 vols (British Library, 2007)

Loyn — H. R. Loyn, "A General introduction to Domesday Book", in A. Williams & R. W. H. Erskine (eds.), *Domesday Book: Studies* (Alecto, 1987)

Luard — H. R. Luard (ed.), *Annales monastici: Annales monasterii de Wintonia* II (Rolls Series 36, 1865)

Lund — Frederick Macody Lund, *Ad Quadratum* I (Batsford, 1921)

MacFarlane & Thomson — Charles MacFarlane & Thomas Thomson, *The Comprehensive History of England* (Blackie, 1876)

Malmesbury — William of Malmesbury, *de gestis pontificum Anglorum* [*c*.1125]: N. E. S. A. Hamilton (ed.), *Willelmi Malmesbiriensis monachi De Gestis Pontificum Anglorum* (Rolls Series 52, 1870), M. Winterbottom & R. M. Thomson (eds.), *William of Malmesbury gesta pontificum Anglorum* I *Text and Translation*, II *Introduction and Commentary* (Clarendon Press, 2007), David Preest (tr.), *William of Malmesbury: The Deeds of the Bishops of England* (Boydell Press, 2002)

Marcay — W. D. Marcay (ed.), *Chronicon abbatiae Ramesiensis* (Rolls Series 83, 1886)

Markuson — K. W. Markuson, "Recent Investigations in the East Range of the Cathedral Monastery, Durham", in Coldstream & Draper, pp. 37-48

Maxwell — Herbert Maxwell (tr.), *The Chronicle of Lanercost* (MacLehose, 1913*)

Moir Boyce	William Moir Boyce, "The Chapel of St Margaret, Edinburgh . . . ", in *The Book of the Old Edinburgh Club* 5 (1912)
Offler, *Charters*	H. S. Offler (ed.), *Durham Episcopal Charters 1071–1152* (Surtees Society 179, 1968)
Offler, *DIV*	H. S. Offler, "The Tractate *De iniusta vexacione Willelmi episcopi primi*", in *English Historical Review* 66 (1951), pp. 321–341
Offler, *William of St Calais*	H. S. Offler, "William of St Calais, First Norman Bishop of Durham", in *Transactions of the Architectural and Archaeological Society of Durham and Northumberland* 10 (1950), pp. 258–80
Orderic Vitalis	Orderic Vitalis, *Ecclesiastical History* [*c.*1141]: Marjorie Chibnall (ed. and tr.), *The Ecclesiastical History of Orderic Vitalis,* 6 vols (Clarendon Press, 1968–80)
Pevsner	Nikolaus Pevsner, *The Buildings of England: County Durham* (Penguin, 1953)
Philpott	Mark Philpott, "The *De inuista uexacione Willelmi episcope primi* and Canon Law in Anglo-Norman Durham", in Rollason, Harvey & Prestwich, pp. 125–137
Powicke	F. M. Powicke, "Maurice of Rievaulx", in *English Historical Review* 36 (1921*), pp. 17–29
Prestwich	J. O. Prestwich, "The Career of Ranulph Flambard", in Rollason, Harvey & Prestwich, pp. 299–310
Raine, *Auckland*	James Raine, *A Brief Historical Account of the Episcopal Castle, or Palace, of Auckland* (Durham, 1852)
Raine, *Cuthbert*	James Raine, *St Cuthbert, with an account of the state in which his remains were found upon the opening of his tomb in Durham Cathedral in the year MDCCCXXVII* (Andrews, 1828*, Nabu Press facsimile reprint on demand)
Raine, *Hexham*	James Raine, *The Priory of Hexham* I (Surtees Society 44, 1864*)
Raine, *Scriptores*	James Raine (ed.), *Historiae Dunelmensis scriptores tres* (Surtees Society 9, 1839*)
Raine, *York*	J. Raine, (ed.), *Historians of the Church of York and its Archbishops* II (Rolls Series 71, 1886*)
Reginald	Reginald of Durham, *Libellus de admirandis Beati Cuthberti virtutibus* [*fl.*1162–1173]: James Raine (ed.), *Reginald of Durham, Libellus de admirandis Beati Cuthberti virtutibus* (Surtees Society 1, 1835*); books xl–xliii translated by Edward G. Pace in Battiscombe, pp. 107–112
Rollason, *Historian*	David Rollason (ed.), "The Making of the *Libellus de exordio*: the Evidence of Erasures and Alterations in the Two Earliest Manuscripts", in *Symeon of Durham*:

	Historian of Durham and the North (Shaun Tyas, 1998), pp. 140–2
Rollason, *LDE*	David Rollason (ed. and tr.), *Libellus de exordio atque procursu istius, hoc est Dunhelmensis, ecclesie* (*Tract on the Origins and Progress of this the Church of Durham*) (Clarendon Press, 2000)
Rollason, *Northumbria*	David W. Rollason, *Northumbria, 500–1100: Creation and Destruction of a Kingdom* (Cambridge University Press, 2003)
Rollason, *Sources*	D. Rollason, "Durham Cathedral 1093–1193: Sources and History", in Jackson, pp. 1–15
Rollason, Harvey & Prestwich	David Rollason, Margaret Harvey & Michael Prestwich (eds.), *Anglo-Norman Durham 1093–1193* (Boydell Press, 1994)
Ronay	Gabriel Ronay, *The Lost King of England: The East European Adventures of Edward the Exile* (Boydell Press, 1989, 2000)
Russo	Thomas E. Russo, "The Romanesque Rood Screen of Durham Cathedral: Context and Form", in Rollason, Harvey & Prestwich, pp. 251–268
Salzman	L. F. Salzman, *Building in England down to 1540: A Documentary History* (Clarendon Press, 1952)
Skene	William F. Skene, *Celtic Scotland* II (Douglas, 1887*)
Snape	M. G. Snape, "Documentary Evidence for the Building of Durham Cathedral", in Coldstream & Draper, pp. 20–36
Stagg	Frank Noel Stagg, *The Heart of Norway* (George Allen & Unwin, 1953)
Stenton	Frank Stenton, *Anglo-Saxon England* (Clarendon Press, 1947 rev. 1971)
Stevenson	Joseph Stevenson (tr.), "The Historical Works of Simeon of Durham", in *The Church Historians of England* III ii (Seeleys, 1855*, Nabu Press facsimile reprint)
Stranks	C. J. Stranks, *This Sumptuous Church: The Story of Durham Cathedral* (SPCK, 1973)
Summerson	Henry Summerson, "Old and New Bishoprics: Durham and Carlisle", in Rollason, Harvey & Prestwich, pp. 369–380
Symeon, *HR*	Symeon of Durham, *Historia regum* [c.1129]: Arnold II, Stevenson
Symeon, *LDE*	Symeon of Durham, *Libellus de exordio atque procursu istius, hoc est Dunhelmensis, ecclesie* [c.1107]: Rollason *LDE*, Arnold I, Stevenson
Talbot, *Christina*	C. H. Talbot (ed. and tr.), *The Life of Christina of Markyate: A Twelfth-Century Recluse* (Oxford University Press, 1959)

Talbot, *Goscelin*   C. H. Talbot, "The *Liber confortatorius* of Goscelin of Saint Bertin", in *Studia Anselmiana* fasc. 37 (Analecta monastica 3rd ser., 1955), pp. 1–117

Thorpe   B. Thorpe (ed.), *Ancient Laws and Institutes of England* I (Comm. Public Records, 1840*)

Thurlby, *Building*   Malcolm Thurlby, "The Building of the Cathedral: the Romanesque and Early Gothic Fabric", in D. C. D. Pocock & Rosalind Billingham (eds.), *Durham Cathedral: A Celebration* (City of Durham Trust, 1993), pp. 15–35

Thurlby, *Mason*   Malcolm Thurlby, "The Roles of the Patron and the Master Mason in the First Design of the Romanesque Cathedral of Durham", in Rollason, Harvey & Prestwich, pp. 161–184

Thurlby, *Rib*   M. Thurlby, "The Purpose of the Rib in the Romanesque Vaults of Durham Cathedral", in Jackson, pp. 64–76

Thurlby, *Vaults*   M. Thurlby, "The Romanesque High Vaults of Durham Cathedral", in Jackson, pp. 43–63

Turgot, *DSM*   "*De Sancta Margareta regina Scotie*", in Carl Horstmann (ed.), *Nova legenda Anglie: as collected by John of Tynemouth, John Capgrave, and others, and first printed, with new lives by Wynkyn de Worde a.d. mdxui*: I (Clarendon Press, 1901*), II (Clarendon Press, 1902*), II, pp. 168–175 [Latin edition of the shorter *Life of St Margaret*]

Turgot, *VSM*   Turgot, *Vita S. Margaretae Scotorum reginae* [*c*.1107]: Anderson II, pp. 59–88, Huneycutt App. II, pp. 161–178, Hinde, pp. 234–254

Van Caenegem   R. C. Van Caenegem, *English Lawsuits from William I to Richard I* I (Selden Society 106, 1990)

VCH I, II & III   *The Victoria History of the Counties of England: A History of Durham* I (Constable, 1905*), II (Constable, 1907*), III (St Catherine Press, 1928*)

Vitruvius   Vitruvius Pollio: Morris H. Morgan (tr.), *The Ten Books on Architecture* (Harvard University Press, 1914*)

Wall   J. Charles Wall, "Pure Norman", in *The Reliquary & Illustrated Archæologist* 12 (1906*), pp. 145–151

Watt   D. E. R. Watt (ed.), *Fasti Ecclesiae Scoticanae medii aevi ad annum 1638* (Scottish Record Society NS 1, 1969)

Wharton   Henry Wharton (ed.), *Anglia Sacra* I (Chiswel, 1691*)

Young   George Young, *A History of Whitby, and Streoneshalh Abbey; with a Statistical Survey of the Vicinity to the Distance of Twenty-five Miles* (Clark and Medd, 1817*)

Zarnecki   George Zarnecki, *Later English Romanesque Sculpture 1140–1210* (Tiranti, 1953)

Notes and References

NB: *s.a. is an abbreviation of* sub anno, *used when quoting annals by the year's entry.*

Introduction

[1]   Blunt p. 428.

1. The Community of St Cuthbert

[1]   Information on Cuthbert is from the works of Bede—*Vita* and *HE*.
[2]   Bede, *Vita* 4: pp. 47–8; *Vita* 6: p. 50; Bede, *HE* iv 27: p. 259. The site of Old Melrose was some 2 miles (3km) east of the present Melrose Abbey, where the embalmed heart of Robert the Bruce is reputedly buried.
[3]   Bede, *Vita* 7: pp. 51–2.
[4]   Bede, *Vita* 7: p. 53 (and p. 51 note 1); Bede, *HE* iii 25: p. 187.
[5]   Bede, *Vita* 39: p. 93.
[6]   Bede, *Vita* 39: p. 93.
[7]   Bede, *Vita* 42: pp. 96–7. It was usual to 'elevate' a saint and re-inter above ground in a new shrine, to enable pilgrims to be close to the relics.
[8]   The cross is now exhibited at the cathedral and the gospel, which was at Stoneyhurst College, Lancs, was purchased in April 2012 by the British Library (Add MS 89000). See also the diagram on p. 48.
[9]   The account in this section is mainly taken from the works of Symeon of Durham—*HR* and *LDE*—based on earlier narratives.
[10]   Symeon, *HR* s.a. 793: Arnold II pp. 54–6, Stevenson pp. 456–8; Symeon, *LDE* ii 5: Rollason, *LDE* pp. 86/7–88/9, Arnold I pp. 50–2, Stevenson pp. 651–2.
[11]   Symeon, *LDE* ii 5: Rollason, *LDE* pp. 92/3 and note 33, Arnold I pp. 52–3, Stevenson p. 653; Symeon, *HR* s.a. 854: Arnold II p. 102, Stevenson p. 486; *HSC*: Arnold I p. 201; Rollason, *Northumbria* p. 215.
[12]   Symeon, *LDE* ii 6: Rollason, *LDE* pp. 98/9, Arnold I pp. 55–6, Stevenson pp. 654–5.
[13]   Symeon, *HR* s.a. 875: Arnold II pp. 82 (nine years), 110 (seven years), Stevenson pp. 475, 493; cf. Symeon *LDE* ii 13: Rollason, *LDE* pp. 120/1, Arnold I p. 68, Stevenson p. 66.
[14]   St Columba's body was removed from Iona to Ireland in 878 in order to avoid Danish invasions.
[15]   Symeon, *LDE* ii 11: Rollason, *LDE* pp. 112/3–114/5, Arnold I p. 64, Stevenson pp. 660–1; *De miraculis* 2: Arnold I pp. 234–7.

[16] Symeon, *LDE* ii 12: Rollason, *LDE* pp. 118/9, Arnold I p. 67, Stevenson pp. 662–3.

[17] Symeon, *LDE* ii 13: Rollason, *LDE* pp. 122/3, Arnold I p. 68, Stevenson p. 664. Crayke provided a residence for the bishop of Lindisfarne on journeys to and from York.

[18] Symeon, *LDE* ii 13: Rollason, *LDE* pp. 122/3–124/5 and note 78, Arnold I pp. 69–70, Stevenson p. 664; Symeon, *HR* s.a. 883: Arnold II p. 86, Stevenson p. 495; *HSC*: Arnold I p. 203.

[19] Cambridge p. 372.

[20] Symeon, *LDE* ii 18: Rollason, *LDE* pp. 134/5–136/7, Arnold I p. 75, Stevenson p. 669.

[21] Most are in the Durham Treasury. The Gospel Book is at the British Library (Cotton. Otho B ix).

[22] Symeon, *LDE* ii 18: Rollason, *LDE* pp. 138/9, Arnold I pp. 76–7, Stevenson p. 670.

[23] Symeon, *LDE* iii 1: Rollason, *LDE* pp. 144/5, Arnold I pp. 78–9, Stevenson p. 671.

[24] *ASC* s.a. 993: p. 144.

[25] Hegge p. 36 summarising Symeon, *LDE* iii 1: Rollason, *LDE* pp. 144/5, Arnold I p. 79, Stevenson pp. 671–2.

[26] Hegge p. 37.

[27] Hegge p. 37.

[28] Symeon, *LDE* iii 2: Rollason, *LDE* pp. 148/9–150/1, Arnold I p. 81, Stevenson p. 673.

[29] See Rollason, *LDE* p. 150 note 11; Rollason, *Sources* pp. 2–3.

[30] Reginald xvi: p. 29, English summary p. 294.

[31] Gem I p. 194 citing Macray p. 41.

[32] Briggs, Cambridge & Bailey pp. 91–7.

[33] Gem I p. 193.

[34] Gem I p. 326 quoting Reginald xvi: p. 29, English summary p. 294.

[35] Johnson p. 111.

[36] Symeon, *LDE* iii 5: Rollason, *LDE* pp. 156/7, Arnold I p. 84, Stevenson pp. 675–6.

[37] Gem I p. 326.

[38] Grid Ref. NZ 432 348.

[39] Symeon, *LDE* iii 8: Rollason, *LDE* pp. 166/7, Arnold I p. 90, Stevenson pp. 679–80.

[40] Symeon, *LDE* iii 9: Rollason, *LDE* pp. 168/9, Arnold I pp. 90–1, Stevenson p. 680.

[41] Symeon, *LDE* iii 9: Rollason, *LDE* pp. 170/1–172/3, Arnold I pp. 90–2, Stevenson pp. 680–1.

[42] Symeon, *LDE* iii 11: Rollason, *LDE* pp. 176/7, Arnold I pp. 94–5, Stevenson p. 683.

[43] Malmesbury iii 115: Preest pp. 167–8.

[44] Symeon, *HR* s.a. 1061: Arnold II pp. 174–5, Stevenson p. 541.

[45] Symeon, *HR* s.a. 1063–5: Arnold II pp. 177–9, Stevenson pp. 543–4; for the causes of the uprising see Freeman II pp. 481–501, Stenton pp. 578–9.

[46] Symeon, *HR* s.a. 1069: Arnold II pp. 186–7, Stevenson p. 550.

[47] Symeon, *LDE* iii 15: Rollason, *LDE* pp. 182/3–184/5, Arnold I pp. 99–100, Stevenson pp. 685–6.

[48] Son of Edward the Exile, grandson of Edmund II Ironside and great-grandson of Æthelred II. His sister Margaret married Malcolm III of Scotland in 1069. The title *ætheling* means throne-worthy from *adel* (noble) *-ing* (youth).

[49] Symeon, *LDE* iii 15: Rollason, *LDE* pp. 186/7, Arnold I p. 100, Stevenson pp. 686–7; Symeon, *HR* s.a. 1069: Arnold II p. 189, Stevenson pp. 551–2; *De miraculis* 6: Hinde pp. 170–2, Arnold I pp. 245–7, Colgrave p. 312.

[50] Symeon, *HR* s.a. 1072: Arnold II pp. 199–200, Stevenson p. 558.

[51] Symeon, *LDE* iii 19: Rollason, *LDE* pp. 196/7, Arnold I p. 106, Stevenson p. 691.

2. Turgot the Traveller

[1] The source for Turgot's life is his fellow-monk Symeon, *HR* s.a. 1074: Latin text in Arnold II pp. 202–5 and a translation in Stevenson pp. 560–561.

[2] The site of the Saxon minster can be deduced from entries made in the Domesday Book at a time when the new cathedral was in course of construction and refers to the site "on which the bishopric now is, **had and has**, the remains of ½ carucate of land". Bishop Remigius also claimed lands given to Bishop Wulfwig (d.1067) and placed in the church of St Mary of Lincoln. (DB Lincs. 336b, city, 17: pp. 882–3 translates the entry as "Of the rest of the land, that is 4½ carucates . . . St Mary of Lincoln, in which the bishopric is now, had and has the remaining half-carucate of land".)

[3] DB—Lincs. 336c; city, 26: p. 883 translate the entry as "Of the aforesaid messuages which were inhabited TRE, there are now waste 200, by English reckoning that is 240; and by the same reckoning 760 are now inhabited . . . Of the aforesaid waste messuages, 166 had been destroyed on account of the castle . . . "

[4] Symeon, *HR* s.a. 1074: Arnold II p. 202, Stevenson p. 560.

[5] Symeon, *HR* s.a. 1074: Arnold II pp. 202–4, Stevenson p. 560. Knowles p. 168 note 1 comments "The reference to the superior English culture is noteworthy".

[6] Stagg p. 22.

[7] Stagg p. 23. (This book has no references or bibliography.)

[8] Hohler pp. 108–9.

[9] Hohler p. 104.

[10] Symeon, *HR* s.a. 1074: Arnold II pp. 202–4, Stevenson p. 560.

[11] ASC s.a. 991: p. 141 (MSS A & G only, s.a. 993, probably a conflation of the entries of 991 and 994).

[12] Battiscombe p. 45.

[13] Michael IV & V and Constantine IX.

[14] The bodyguard of the Byzantine emperors was formed partly of Norse sea-rovers (Varangians).

[15] Lund I p. 198.

[16] Hohler p. 109.

[17] Hohler p. 95.

[18] Named *Ecclesia Sanctae Trinitatis* in the Domesday survey of 1086. DB Kent.

[19] Hohler pp. 104 notes 2 and 108.

[20] Atkinson p. 1; Young p. 243.

[21] Symeon, *HR* s.a. 1074: Arnold II p. 201, Stevenson p. 559; Symeon, *LDE* iii 21: Rollason, *LDE* pp. 200/1–204/5, Arnold I pp. 108–9, Stevenson pp. 692–4.

[22] Symeon, *HR* s.a. 1069: Arnold II p. 189, Stevenson p. 552.

[23] Symeon, *LDE* iii 22: Rollason, *LDE* pp. 206/7, Arnold I p. 111, Stevenson p. 694.

[24] Symeon, *LDE* iii 21: Rollason, *LDE* pp. 202/3, Arnold I p. 109, Stevenson p. 693.

[25] Offler, *Charters* pp. 3, 4.

[26] "*Ingenio acutus, consilio prouidus ... semper celestia desiderans, et secum quoscunque poterat illuc prouocans*": Symeon, *LDE* iii 21: Rollason, *LDE* pp. 204/5, Arnold I p. 110, Stevenson pp. 693–4.

[27] Symeon, *LDE* iii 21: Rollason, *LDE* pp. 202/3, Arnold I pp. 109–10, Stevenson p. 693.

[28] Atkinson p. 1; Young p. 243.

[29] Anderson II pp. 38 and 59 note 1 quoting Hoveden: Stubbs I p. 59.

[30] Symeon, *LDE* iii 22: Rollason, *LDE* pp. 208/9, Arnold I p. 112, Stevenson p. 695.

[31] Symeon, *HR* s.a. 1070: Arnold II pp. 190–1, Stevenson p. 553.

[32] Symeon, *LDE* iii 22: Rollason, *LDE* pp. 208/9–210/11, Arnold I p. 113, Stevenson pp. 695–6.

[33] Symeon, *LDE* iii 22: Rollason, *LDE* pp. 208/9, Arnold I p. 112, Stevenson p. 695; referring to Matthew 11:30.

[34] Symeon, *LDE* iii 22: Rollason, *LDE* pp. 210/11, Arnold I p. 113, Stevenson p. 696.

[35] Symeon, *LDE* iii 22: Rollason, *LDE* pp. 208/9, Arnold I p. 112, Stevenson p. 695.

[36] Symeon, *LDE* iii 18: Rollason, *LDE* pp. 194/5, Arnold I p. 105, Stevenson p. 690.

[37] Symeon, *LDE* iii 22: Rollason, *LDE* pp. 210/11, Arnold I p. 113, Stevenson p. 696.

[38] Symeon, *LDE* iii 23: Rollason, *LDE* pp. 212/13, Arnold I p. 114, Stevenson p. 696; Symeon, *HR* s.a. 1074 & 1075: Arnold II pp. 205–7, Stevenson pp. 562–3.

[39] Symeon, *HR* s.a. 1080: Arnold II pp. 209/10, Stevenson p. 565; cf. Symeon, *LDE* iii 23: Rollason, *LDE* pp. 212/13, Arnold I p. 114, Stevenson p. 696.

[40] Symeon, *LDE* iii 24: Rollason, *LDE* pp. 216/7–218/9, Arnold I pp. 116–7, Stevenson pp. 698–9; Symeon, *HR* s.a. 1080: Arnold II p. 210, Stevenson pp. 565–6.

[41] Symeon, *LDE* iii 24: Rollason, *LDE* pp. 218/9, Arnold I p. 118, Stevenson pp. 699.

[42] Symeon, *LDE* iv 1: Rollason, *LDE* pp. 222/3, Arnold I p. 119, Stevenson pp. 699–700; in Symeon, *HR* s.a. 1080: Arnold II p. 211, Stevenson p. 566, the date is given as the fourth of the nones of January (2 January). For the career of Bishop William see Aird, *William of St Calais*; Offler, *William of St Calais*.

[43] Offler, *William of St Calais* p. 262 note 13; Symeon, *LDE* iv 1: Rollason, *LDE* pp. 222/3, Arnold I p. 119, Stevenson pp. 699–700.

[44] Offler, *Charters* p. 63.

[45] Symeon, *LDE* iv 5: Rollason, *LDE* pp. 236/7, Arnold I p. 125, Stevenson p. 704.

[46] Davis I p. 146: Index of Persons: Durham, Bishops of: William.

[47] Malmesbury i 49: Preest p. 58.

[48] Symeon, *LDE* iv 2: Rollason, *LDE* pp. 224/5–226/7, Arnold I p. 120, Stevenson p. 700.

[49] Symeon, *HR* s.a. 1080: Arnold II pp. 210–11, Stevenson p. 566; Symeon, *LDE* iii 24: Rollason, *LDE* pp. 218/9, Arnold p. 118, Stevenson p. 699.

[50] Raine, *Cuthbert* pp. 70–72.

[51] Symeon, *LDE* iv 2: Rollason, *LDE* pp. 226/7 and note 14, Arnold I p. 121, Stevenson p. 701.

[52] Symeon, *LDE* iii 2: Rollason, *LDE* pp. 148/9, Arnold I p. 81, Stevenson p. 673.

[53] Knowles p. 625.

[54] Symeon, *LDE* iv 3: Rollason, *LDE* pp. 230/1, Arnold I pp. 122–3, Stevenson p. 702.

[55] Symeon, *LDE* iv 3: Rollason, *LDE* pp. 230/1 note *e* & note 20, Arnold I p. 123 note *a*, Stevenson p. 702 note 6.

[56] Rollason, *LDE* p. lxxxix; Raine, *Hexham* I pp. lii–lx.

[57] Symeon, *LDE* iv 3: Rollason, *LDE* pp. 230/1, Arnold I p. 122 (cf. Stevenson p. 702 note 3); The names of the first 230 monks of Durham are listed at the beginning of *LDE*. The first 23 named are Aldwin, Elfwy, William, Leofwin, Wulmar, Turgot, Edwin, Turkill, Gregory, Columbanus, Elfwin, Godwin, Elmar, Elias, Swartbrand, Gamel, Godwin, Wiking, Godwin, Ailric, Seulf, Edmund and Robert: Rollason *LDE* pp. 6/7, Arnold I pp. 4–5.

[58] Symeon, *LDE* iv 3: Rollason, *LDE* pp. 232/3, Arnold I p. 123, Stevenson p. 703. There is no mention of the sub-prior Turgot, who may have been the source for this section.

[59] Symeon, *LDE* iv 3: Rollason, *LDE* pp. 232/3, Arnold I p. 123, Stevenson p. 703.

[60] ASC s.a. 1086: p. 213; cf. Symeon, *HR* s.a. 1086: Arnold II p. 213, Stevenson p. 567.

[61] The suggestion that the bishop was the brain behind the survey was first made by R. W. Eyton, *A Key to Domesday Exemplified by the Dorset Survey* (1878).

[62] Loyn p. 7.

[63] Expression coined by Galbraith p. 50.

[64] Chaplais p. 74.

[65] Symeon, *HR* s.a. 1086: Arnold II p. 213, Stevenson p. 567.

[66] DB *Exoniensis* E 31/2 fol.175v; Great Domesday fol. 87v: *DB* p. 235.

[67] DB Notts. 291c, Lincs. 337a, 347b, 351a, 352, 353d, 366a.

3. Turgot the Prior

[1] Symeon, *LDE* iv 7: Rollason, *LDE* pp. 240/1, Arnold I p. 127, Stevenson p. 705.

[2] "*In cuius locum iure prioratus discipulum illius uidelicet Turgotum*": Symeon, *LDE* iv 7: Rollason, *LDE* pp. 240/1, Arnold I p. 127, Stevenson p. 705.

[3] Fowler, *Rites* pp. 44–5.

[4] Fowler, *Rites* pp. 105–6 and notes on pp. 287–8.

[5] Lund I p. 249.

[6] Symeon, *LDE* iv 5–6: Rollason, *LDE* pp. 238/9–240/1, Arnold I pp. 125–6, Stevenson pp. 704–5.

[7] Hutchinson II p. 65.

[8] Fowler, *Rites* p. 83.

[9] *De miraculis* 12: Hinde pp. 180–1, Arnold II pp. 345–7, Colgrave p. 315.

[10] Symeon, *LDE* iv 4: Rollason, *LDE* pp. 234/5–236/7, Arnold I pp. 124–5, Stevenson pp. 703–4.

[11] Dean and Chapter Muniments I.I Pont 2b: Davis I no. 148.

[12] Malmesbury iii 133: Preest p. 183.

[13] *DIV*: Arnold I pp. 170–95, Stevenson pp. 731–750.

[14] No doubt the Durham copy now at Cambridge (Peterhouse College MS 74); see Philpott p. 131.

[15] *DIV*: Arnold I p. 188, Stevenson p. 744.

[16] *DIV*: Arnold I pp. 191–2, Stevenson p. 747, Offler, *DIV* p. 323.

[17] Van Caenegem I p. 100.

[18] Symeon, *LDE* iv 8: Rollason, *LDE* pp. 242/3, Arnold I p. 128, Stevenson p. 706.

[19] *DIV*: Arnold I pp. 194–5, Stevenson p. 749.

[20] Symeon, *LDE* iv 8: Rollason, *LDE* pp. 242/3, Arnold I p. 128, Stevenson p. 706.

[21] *De miraculis* 10: Hinde pp. 177–8, Arnold II pp. 341–3, Colgrave p. 314.

[22] Bilson, *Discoveries* p. 16; Hutchinson I (1786) p. 137, (1823) p. 166, II p. 63; see Symeon, *LDE* iv 8: Rollason, *LDE* pp. 242/3, Arnold I p. 128, Stevenson p. 706.

[23] Reginald lxxxi: pp. 169–170, English summary p. 310.

[24] Symeon, *HR* s.a. 1092: Arnold II pp. 221–2, Stevenson p. 573; cf. Symeon, *HR* s.a. 1091: Arnold II p. 218, Stevenson p. 571.

[25] Symeon, *LDE* iv 8: Rollason, *LDE* pp. 242/3, Arnold I p. 128, Stevenson p. 706; Symeon, *HR* s.a. 1091: Arnold II p. 218, Stevenson p. 571.

[26] Anderson, *Annals* p. 107, quoting Orderic Vitalis viii 20; (cf. Symeon, *HR* s.a. 1091: Arnold II p. 218, Stevenson p. 571).

[27] Symeon, *HR* s.a. 1092: Arnold II p. 220, Stevenson p. 572 ; *ASC* s.a. 1093: p. 230.

[28] Symeon, *HR* s.a. 1091: Arnold II p. 218, Stevenson p. 571; *DIV*: Arnold I p. 195, Stevenson p. 749; David p. 386; Craster H p. 35.

[29] Symeon, *LDE* iv 8: Rollason, *LDE* pp. 244/5, Arnold I p. 128, Stevenson p. 706.

[30] Botfield pp. 117–8, 195.

[31] Hutchinson I (1785) p. 138, (1823) p. 168; Devonshire & Wilkie pp. 17–18.

[32] Symeon, *LDE* iv 8: Rollason, *LDE* pp. 244/5, Arnold I p. 129, Stevenson p. 707; see Summerson p. 369.

[33] Hutchinson II p. 8; I (1785) p. 134, (1823) p. 163; *VCH* III p. 61; *Liber Vitae* 53r1, 53v1, 54r1: II pp. 156–7; Offler, *Charters* no. 3 pp. 6–9.

[34] Davis I nos. 330, 331, 332.

[35] Hutchinson II p. 63.

[36] Lund I p. 246.

[37] Fowler, *Rites* p. 72.

[38] *DIV*: Arnold I p. 195, Stevenson p. 749.

[39] Rollason, *Sources* p. 6.

[40] Fowler, *Rites* p. 74.

[41] Fowler, *Rites* pp. 68–9, 73, 74–5, 137–43, 251.

[42] Kjolbye-Biddle p. 196.

[43] Talbot, *Goscelin* p. 93.

[44] Briggs, Cambridge & Bailey pp. 91–7.

[45] Symeon, *LDE* iv 8: Rollason, *LDE* pp. 244/5, Arnold I p. 129, Stevenson p. 707.

[46] Bilson, *Discoveries* pp. 6, 8; contrast Johnson pp. 116–9.

[47] Symeon, *LDE* iv 8: Rollason, *LDE* pp. 244/5–246/7, Arnold I p. 129, Stevenson p. 707.

[48] Malmesbury iii 133: Preest p. 184.

[49] Symeon, *LDE* iv 8: Rollason, *LDE* pp. 246/7, Arnold I p. 129, Stevenson p. 707.

[50] See p. 6; Craster E p. 181; Summerson p. 370.

[51] Davis I nos. 463, 478; see Summerson p. 370.

[52] Symeon, *HR* s.a. 1072: Arnold II p. 198, Stevenson p. 557.

[53] Symeon, *HR* s.a. 1072: Arnold II p. 198, Stevenson p. 557.

[54] *Liber Vitae* 52v3: II pp. 155–6.

[55] Symeon, *HR* s.a. 1093: Arnold II p. 220, Stevenson p. 573; *DIV*: Arnold I p. 195, Stevenson p. 750; (cf. Symeon, *LDE* iv 8: Rollason, *LDE* pp. 244/5, Arnold I p. 129, Stevenson p. 707).

[56] Anderson, *Annals* p. 110, quoting Florence: Thorpe II p. 31; (cf. Symeon, *HR* s.a. 1093: Arnold II pp. 220–1, Stevenson p. 573).

[57] Davis I no. 336.

[58] Johnson & Cronne II p. 401 no. 338a.

[59] Johnson & Cronne II p. 401 no. 348a.

[60] Malmesbury i 49 records that the bishop instigated the quarrel between the king and Anselm, hoping to make his way into the archbishopric if Anselm was deposed: Preest p. 58.

[61] Davis I no. 363 (cf. nos. 364–365 and notes to 363).

[62] Symeon, *HR* s.a. 1095: Arnold II p. 225, Stevenson p. 577.

[63] Symeon, *LDE* iv 10: Rollason, *LDE* pp. 252/3, Arnold I p. 133, Stevenson pp. 710–11.

[64] Raine, *Auckland* p. 8.

[65] Van Caenegem p. 106.

[66] Raine, *Auckland* p. 8 note 1 states that the grave was opened in 1795 and revealed the bones of a tall man, portions of sandals, and fragments of a robe richly embroidered in gold, ornamented with griffins *passant*, and other quaint devices.

[67] Symeon, *LDE* iv 10: Rollason, *LDE* pp. 256/7, Arnold I p. 134, Stevenson p. 711.

[68] Aird, *William of St Calais* pp. 286–7.

[69] Symeon, *LDE* iv 9: Rollason, *LDE* pp. 246/7–250/1, Arnold I pp. 130–2, Stevenson pp. 707–709.

[70] Symeon, *LDE* iv 10: Rollason, *LDE* pp. 250/1–252/3, Arnold I pp. 132–3, Stevenson pp. 709–711.

[71] Symeon, *LDE* iv 5: Rollason, *LDE* pp. 238/9, Arnold I p. 125, Stevenson p. 704.

[72] Symeon, *LDE* iv 3: Rollason, *LDE* pp. 234/5, Arnold I p. 123, Stevenson p. 703.

[73] Davis I no. 396.

[74] Davis I no. 478; Craster H p. 38.

[75] *LDE Cont* i: Rollason, *LDE* pp. 266/7, Arnold I p. 135, Stevenson p. 712.

[76] Malmesbury iii 134: Hamilton p. 274 note 3, Winterbottom & Thomson I pp. 416–7.

[77] Symeon, *HR* s.a. 1099: Arnold II p. 230, Stevenson p. 580.

[78] For the career of Ranulf Flambard see Prestwich.

[79] Symeon, *LDE* iii 14: Rollason, *LDE* pp. 180/1, Arnold I p. 97, Stevenson p. 685.

[80] *LDE Cont* i: Rollason, *LDE* pp. 274/5, Arnold I p. 139, Stevenson p. 715; see Summerson p. 370.

[81] *LDE Cont* ii: Rollason, *LDE* pp. 276/7, Arnold I p. 140, Stevenson p. 715.

[82] Snape p. 21.

[83] Orderic Vitalis iii 311: Chibnall IV p. 172.
[84] Prestwich p. 308 citing Luard II p. 39.
[85] Anselm: Schmitt iv 113.
[86] *LDE Cont* i: Rollason, *LDE* pp. 266/7, Arnold I p. 135, Stevenson p. 712.
[87] Malmesbury iii 134: Hamilton p. 274 note 3, Winterbottom & Thomson pp. 416/7.
[88] Florence: Thorpe II p. 44, Stevenson pp. 320–1.
[89] *LDE Cont* i: Rollason, *LDE* pp. 272/3, Arnold I p. 138, Stevenson p. 714; Symeon, *HR* s.a. 1099: Arnold II p. 230, Stevenson p. 580 (who misread it as St *Peter's* church—i.e. Westminster Abbey).
[90] Orderic Vitalis x 310–13: Chibnall V pp. 310/11–312/13.
[91] Johnson & Cronne II nos. 544–6, 548.
[92] Orderic Vitalis: Chibnall IV pp. 116/7.
[93] Prestwich p. 301 citing Talbot, *Christina* pp. 40–42.
[94] Prestwich p. 301 citing Luard II pp. 47–8.
[95] *LDE Cont* ii: Rollason, *LDE* pp. 278/9, Arnold I p. 141, Stevenson pp. 716–7.
[96] *LDE Cont* ii: Rollason, *LDE* pp. 278/9, Arnold I p. 140, Stevenson p. 715. '*Caniculares dies*'—during the combined heat of sun and dog-star, i.e. early July to mid August.
[97] Fowler, *Excavations* pp. 385–404.
[98] *LDE Cont* i: Rollason, *LDE* pp. 274/5, Arnold I p. 139, Stevenson p. 715.

4. Turgot the Servant of St Cuthbert

[1] Turgot, *VSM* Introduction: Anderson II p. 59 (see Chapters 6 and 7).
[2] The following manuscripts contain all the later miracles: Trinity College, Cambridge: Gale 0.3.55 (12th century); Durham Cathedral Muniments: A IV 35 (late 12th century); British Library: Add. MS 39943 (late 12th century); Arundel MS 332 (13th century), Harleian MS 4843 (early 16th century); Bodleian Library Oxford: Fairfax 6 (3886) (14th century). The Latin texts have been published in Hinde pp. 158–201, and Arnold I pp. 229–61 and II pp. 333–362. A summary of each is included in Colgrave.
[3] Symeon, *LDE* iii 19: Rollason, *LDE* pp. 196/7, Arnold I p. 106, Stevenson p. 691: see p. 12.
[4] Symeon, *LDE* iii 20: Rollason, *LDE* pp. 196/7–198/9, Arnold I p. 107, Stevenson pp. 691–2.
[5] Powicke pp. 20–1.
[6] Hinde pp. 158–62, Arnold I pp. 229–34, Colgrave p. 310; Malmesbury iii 130: Preest pp. 180–1.
[7] Hinde pp. 162–4, Arnold I pp. 234–7, Colgrave p. 310.
[8] Hinde pp. 165–6, Arnold I pp. 238–40, Colgrave p. 311.
[9] Hinde pp. 167–8, Arnold I pp. 240–2, Colgrave p. 311.
[10] Hinde pp. 168–70, Arnold I pp. 243–5, Colgrave p. 312.
[11] Hinde pp. 170–2, Arnold I pp. 245–7, Colgrave p. 312.
[12] Hinde pp. 172–3, Arnold II pp. 333–5, Colgrave p. 313.

[13] Hinde pp. 173–5, Arnold II pp. 335–8, Colgrave p. 313.

[14] Hinde pp. 175–7, Arnold II pp. 338–41, Colgrave p. 313.

[15] Hinde pp. 177–8, Arnold II pp. 341–3, Colgrave p. 314.

[16] Hinde pp. 178–9, Arnold II pp. 343–4, Colgrave p. 314.

[17] Hinde pp. 180–1, Arnold II pp. 345–7, Colgrave p. 315.

[18] Hinde pp. 181–2, Arnold II pp. 347–8, Colgrave p. 315.

[19] Hinde pp. 182–3, Arnold II pp. 348–50, Colgrave p. 315.

[20] Hinde pp. 183–5, Arnold II pp. 350–2, Colgrave p. 316.

[21] Hinde pp. 185–6, Arnold II pp. 352–3, Colgrave p. 316.

[22] Hinde pp. 186–8, Arnold II pp. 353–6, Colgrave p. 316.

[23] Hinde pp. 188–97, Arnold I pp. 247–61, Colgrave p. 317.

[24] Hinde pp. 197–8, Arnold II pp. 359–61, Colgrave p. 317.

[25] Hinde pp. 198–9, Arnold II pp. 361–2, Colgrave p. 318.

[26] Hinde pp. 199–201, Arnold II pp. 356–9, Colgrave p. 318.

[27] Fowler, *Rites* pp. 68, 73, 74–5, 140, 251; Crook pp. 240–1; Briggs, Cambridge & Bailey pp. 91–7.

[28] Malmesbury iii 135: Hamilton p. 275, Preest p. 185, Winterbottom & Thomson I p. 419.

[29] Battiscombe p. 45 remarks that it would have been strange if Turgot never repeated such a tale to his monks.

[30] Symeon, *HR* s.a. 1104: Arnold II pp. 236–7, Stevenson pp. 585–6.

[31] Reginald xl: p. 84, Battiscombe p. 107.

[32] Battiscombe p. 56; *De miraculis* 18: Hinde I pp. 188–197, Arnold I pp. 247–61; translation by R. A. B. Mynors in Battiscombe pp. 99–107, based on Raine, *Cuthbert* pp. 74–85.

[33] Reginald xl: p. 84, Battiscombe p. 107; Reginald's account is in Reginald xl–xliii: pp. 84–91; translation by E. G. Pace in Battiscombe pp. 107–112, Stevenson pp. 779–785.

[34] Battiscombe p. 100.

[35] Battiscombe pp. 111, 103.

[36] Battiscombe p. 101.

[37] Battiscombe p. 101.

[38] Battiscombe p. 102.

[39] Battiscombe p. 102.

[40] Battiscombe pp. 102, 107.

[41] The bones that were transferred to a different part of the church included those of Bede (d.735), St Aidan (d.651), and two bishops of Lindisfarne, Eadfrid (d.721) and Ethelwaldus (d.740). It was not until 1370 that the remains of Bede were interred in the galilee at the west end of Durham Cathedral, built about 1170.

[42] Battiscombe p. 102.

[43] Battiscombe p. 103.

[44] Battiscombe p. 103.

[45] Battiscombe p. 103.

[46] Battiscombe p. 104.

[47] Ralph d'Escures (d.1122) became archbishop of Canterbury in 1114.

[48] Farrer p. 26.

[49] Battiscombe p. 105.

[50] Battiscombe p. 105; William de Corbeil (d.1135) became archbishop of Canterbury in 1123.

[51] Battiscombe p. 106.

[52] Battiscombe p. 106.

[53] Fowler, *Rites* p. 103.

[54] Raine, *Cuthbert* pp. 183–216; see also *VCH* I pp. 241–258.

[55] Raine, *Cuthbert* PLATES I–VIII; see also *VCH* I pp. 241–258; Battiscombe pp. 202–256. The silk now known as the 'Nature Goddess Silk' has been reinterpreted since Raine's drawing was made—see Battiscombe pp. 10, 505–513.

[56] *VCH* I pp. 252–4; Battiscombe pp. 92–8.

[57] Battiscombe p. 106.

[58] Malmesbury iii 134: Hamilton p. 274, Preest p. 185, Winterbottom & Thomson I p. 419.

[59] Battiscombe p. 106.

[60] Florence s.a. 1104: Stevenson p. 326, Thorpe II p. 53.

[61] *De miraculis* 19: Arnold II pp. 359–61.

[62] Crook p. 249 citing Reginald xlv: p. 92, English summary p. 300.

[63] Crook p. 249 citing Reginald cxiv: p. 259, English summary pp. 319–20.

[64] Crook p. 249 citing Offler, *Charters* pp. 112–4, Fowler, *Rites* p. 4.

[65] *De miraculis* 19: Hinde pp. 197–8, Arnold II pp. 359–61.

[66] *De miraculis* 20: Hinde pp. 198–9, Arnold II pp. 361–2.

[67] See pp. 11, 52–3: Oxford, Bodleian Library, University College MS 165; and see Baker.

[68] See Fowler, *Rites* notes p. 284.

[69] Johnson & Cronne II nos. 683, 699.

[70] Johnson & Cronne II no. 887.

[71] Offler, *Charters* nos. 17, 20, 24, 25.

[72] Craster H no. XIX p. 49 .

[73] *LDE Cont* i: Rollason, *LDE* pp. 274/5, Arnold I pp. 139–40, Stevenson p. 715.

[74] *LDE Cont* ii: Rollason, *LDE* pp. 276/7–278/9, Arnold I p. 140, Stevenson p. 716.

[75] Eadmer suggests he may have been selected as early as 1107: p. 198; (cf. Symeon, *HR* s.a.1074: Arnold II p. 204, Stevenson p. 561. See also Dowden p. 1).

[76] Hinde p. 96 note *q* quoting Eadmer: p. 198.

[77] Eadmer: pp. 198–9.

[78] Hoveden: Stubbs p. 261, Riley p. 203: "On the calends of August, being Sunday"; Stevenson p. 589 & note 2 (Symeon, *HR* s.a.1109) says Sunday 30 July (the third of the calends of August) but 30 July fell upon a Friday. This is due to a misreading of "*in*" as "*iii*" by Twysden, whose edition Stevenson used. Arnold II p. 241 also has "*iii*", but has a note stating that Florence reads "*in kal*".

[79] Ephesians 2:6.

[80] Bilson, *Chronology* p. 137.

[81] *LDE Cont* ii: Rollason, *LDE* pp. 276/7, Arnold I p. 140, Stevenson p. 715.

[82] Clapham II p. 59 note.

[83] Ferrey p. 609.

[84] Ferrey p. 608.

[85] *LDE Cont* ii: Rollason, *LDE* pp. 280/1, Arnold I p. 141, Stevenson p. 717.

[86] Ferrey p. 609.

[87] *LDE Cont* ii: Rollason, *LDE* pp. 276/7, Arnold I p. 140, Stevenson p. 716.

[88] *LDE Cont* ii: Rollason, *LDE* pp. 276/7, Arnold I p. 140, Stevenson p. 716.

5. Turgot the Builder

[1] Blunt p. 427.

[2] Bilson, *Chronology* p. 159.

[3] Dosseret: This French term normally refers to an additional high block or slab set on top of an abacus (the flat slab on the top of the capital of a column), between it and the spandrel of the arch above, and is also called a super-abacus: Fleming, Honour & Pevsner p. 19. However, the usage here seems rather to suggest a flat panel behind the half-shaft extending a little way on either side of it.

[4] Gem & Thurlby p. 38.

[5] Wall p. 145.

[6] Bony, *Stonework* p. 19.

[7] Bony, *Stonework* pp. 25–34.

[8] Gem II p. 562.

[9] Symeon, *LDE* iv 8: Rollason, *LDE* pp. 244/5, Arnold I p. 129, Stevenson p. 707.

[10] Thurlby, *Mason* p. 161.

[11] Thurlby, *Mason* p. 183.

[12] Bilson, *Chronology* p. 108.

[13] Thurlby, *Mason* p. 184.

[14] Bony, *Stonework* p. 26.

[15] Bony, *Stonework* p. 24.

[16] Bony, *Stonework* p. 25 and p. 26.

[17] Bony, *Stonework* pp. 29–30.

[18] Bony, *Stonework* p. 29.

[19] Bilson, *Vaults*; Bilson, *Chronology*.

[20] Bony, *French Gothic* p. 10.

[21] Bilson, *Chronology* p. 109.

[22] Symeon, *LDE* iii 22: Rollason, *LDE* pp. 210/11, Arnold I p. 113, Stevenson p. 696.

[23] Symeon, *LDE* iv 8: Rollason, *LDE* pp. 242/3, Arnold I p. 128, Stevenson p. 706; Bilson, *Discoveries* p. 16; Hutchinson I (1786) p. 137, (1823) p. 166, II p. 63; Rollason, *Sources* p. 6.

[24] Symeon, *LDE* iv 8: Rollason, *LDE* pp. 244/5, Arnold I pp. 128–9, Stevenson pp. 706–7; *DIV*: Arnold I p. 195, Stevenson p. 749.

[25] Symeon, *LDE* iv 8: Rollason, *LDE* pp. 244/5, Arnold I p. 129, Stevenson p. 707.

[26] Symeon, *LDE* iv 8: Rollason, *LDE* pp. 244/5, Arnold I p. 129, Stevenson p. 707; Symeon, *HR* s.a. 1093: Arnold II p. 220, Stevenson p. 573; *DIV*: Arnold I p. 195, Stevenson p. 750.

[27] Bilson, *Discoveries* pp. 6, 8; contrast Johnson G pp. 116–9.

[28] Bilson, *Chronology* p. 159.

[29] *LDE Cont* i: Rollason, *LDE* pp. 276/7, Arnold I pp. 139–40, Stevenson p. 715.

[30] Thurlby, *Vaults* pp. 45–6.

[31] Bilson, *Chronology* pp. 138–140.

[32] *LDE Cont* ii: Rollason, *LDE* pp. 274/5–276/7, Arnold I p. 139, Stevenson p. 715; the word *testudinem* is derived from a tortoise shell.

[33] *LDE Cont* ii: Rollason, *LDE* pp. 280/1, Arnold I p. 141, Stevenson p. 717.

[34] Zarnecki.

[35] *LDE Cont* iii: Rollason, *LDE* pp. 282/3, Arnold I p. 142, Stevenson p. 718; Snape p. 22.

[36] Snape p. 22 citing *LDE Cont* (only in Cambridge, University Library, Ff. i.27): Rollason, *LDE* pp. 320/1, Arnold I p. 167.

[37] Snape p. 23.

[38] Coldingham: pp. 11–12.

[39] Snape p. 23 citing Greenwell, *Feodarium* pp. 237–8.

[40] Snape p. 24 citing Fowler, *Rites* pp. 149–50.

[41] *VCH* III p. 94 citing Graystanes: p. 42.

[42] Snape pp. 25–6 citing Raine, *Scriptores* App. 29 pp. xlvii–xlviii.

[43] Snape p. 24.

[44] Snape p. 26 citing Graystanes: p. 46.

[45] Snape pp. 24–5.

[46] Snape p. 26 citing Graystanes: p. 77.

[47] Details of expenses are summarised in Fowler, *Accounts* pp. 569–574 and in Raine, *Scriptores* pp. 132–3 note †; see also Greenwell, *Cathedral* p. 79; Snape p. 27.

[48] Greenwell, *Cathedral* p. 61 citing Chambre: pp. 135–6; Snape pp. 26–7.

[49] The contract with the mason is printed in Raine, *Scriptores* App. 160 pp. clxxx–clxxxii; Hills p. 234; Snape p. 28.

[50] *VCH* III p. 124 citing Chambre: pp. 145–6; Fowler, *Rites* p. 76; Snape pp. 29–30.

[51] *VCH* III p. 125; Snape p. 30; Markuson p. 37 citing Fowler, *Accounts* p. 46.

[52] Snape p. 30.

[53] Raine, *Scriptores* App. 193 pp. ccxvii–ccxviii; Hills p. 210; Snape p. 31.

[54] Snape p. 31.

[55] *VCH* III p. 128 note 55a citing Hope & Fowler p. 452; Fowler, *Rites* pp. 82–3; Snape p. 30.

[56] Snape p. 32.

[57] Thurlby, *Vaults* pp. 44–6.

[58] Bilson, *Discoveries* p. 5.

[59] Bilson, *Discoveries* p. 13.

[60] Snape pp. 23–4 citing Fowler, *Rites* pp. 149–150; Thurlby, *Vaults* p. 43.

[61] Thurlby, *Vaults* p. 47.

[62] Thurlby, *Vaults* p. 43.

[63] Bilson, *Discoveries* p. 5.

[64] Bilson, *Discoveries* p. 15.

[65] Thurlby, *Vaults* p. 49.

[66] Thurlby, *Vaults* pp. 52–3.

[67] Thurlby, *Vaults* p. 53.

[68] Bilson, *Chronology* pp. 128–9, 137, 138, 160; see also Thurlby, *Vaults* pp. 47–55.

[69] *LDE Cont* ii: Rollason, *LDE* pp. 274/5–276/7, Arnold I pp. 139–40, Stevenson p. 715.

[70] Strank p. 32.

[71] Vitruvius iii 5: p. 96.

[72] BL Harleian 2767.

[73] Borg p. 130.

[74] Thurlby, *Vaults* p. 56; contrast Bilson, *Chronology* p. 143.

[75] Thurlby, *Vaults* p. 58; Bilson, *Chronology* pp. 143–4.

[76] Thurlby, *Vaults* p. 58; contrast Bilson, *Chronology* pp. 143–4.

[77] Ferrey p. 608.

[78] *LDE Cont* ii: Rollason, *LDE* pp. 280/1, Arnold I p. 141, Stevenson p. 717.

[79] Bilson, *Discoveries* p. 2; (cf. Thurlby, *Vaults* p. 56).

[80] *LDE Cont* iii: Rollason, *LDE* pp. 282/3, Arnold I p. 142, Stevenson p. 718.

[81] Pevsner p. 77.

[82] Symeon, *LDE* iii 22: Rollason, *LDE* pp. 210/11, Arnold I p. 113, Stevenson p. 696.

[83] Hope & Fowler p. 416.

[84] *VCH* III p. 123 citing Hope p. 416.

[85] *LDE Cont* ii: Rollason, *LDE* pp. 276/7, Arnold I p. 140, Stevenson p. 716.

[86] Hope pp. 417–423.

[87] Sixteenth-century descriptions of the claustral buildings and their use immediately before the Reformation can be found in Fowler, *Rites* pp. 63–89 with notes on pp. 247–270.

[88] Briggs, Cambridge & Bailey pp. 91–7, citing Fowler, *Rites* pp. 68–9, 74–5, 137–43, 251; Reginald: pp. xvii, 100.

[89] Markuson pp. 37–48; *VCH* III p. 126; Fowler, *Rites* pp. 56, 243. 91 Symeon, *LDE* iv 8: Rollason, *LDE* pp. 242/3, Arnold I p. 128, Stevenson p. 706; Bilson, *Discoveries* p. 16; Hutchinson I (1786) p. 137, (1823) p. 166, II p. 63; Rollason, *Sources* p. 6.

[90] All attempts to trace the copyright holder of the original drawing, which was published in James Wall, *Durham Cathedral* (J. M. Dent Sons Ltd, 1930) p. 35, have been unsuccessful.

[92] Hills p. 231.

[93] Gee p. 73.

[94] Hills pp. 229–30; *VCH* III p. 134; Pocock p. 15; Markuson pp. 37, 40–1, 43–6.

[95] Markuson p. 39.

[96] *VCH* III p. 130; Hills p. 233; Fowler, *Rites* p. 265.

[97] Hope p. 417.

[98] Snape p. 22 citing *LDE Cont* (only in Cambridge, University Library, Ff. i.27): Rollason, *LDE* pp. 320/1, Arnold I p. 167.

[99] *LDE Cont* iii: Rollason, *LDE* pp. 280/1–282/3, Arnold I p. 142, Stevenson p. 718; Markuson p. 39 citing Greenwell, *Cathedral* (1904) pp. 40, 47 and note, 53.

[100] Hope p. 420.

[101] Bilson, *Chronology* p. 159.

[102] Markuson p. 37. In the sixteenth century it was also used for trade—"a place for merchauntes to vtter ther waires": Fowler, *Rites* p. 52.

[103] *VCH* III p. 125; Snape p. 30; Markuson p. 37 citing Fowler, *Accounts* p. 46.

[104] Clark pp. 154–5.

[105] Hope & Fowler pp. 437–460.

[106] Hope & Fowler p. 453.

[107] Fowler, *Accounts* p. 536.

[108] Hope & Fowler pp. 448–9, 458–60, citing Raine, *Scriptores* App. 346 p. ccccxliii.

[109] Fowler, *Rites* pp. 82–3; see also *VCH* III p. 128 note 55a citing Hope & Fowler p. 452.

6. Turgot the Writer

[1] Wharton I pp. xlvii–xlviii, 691ff (marginal notes), 705, citing Selden, *Historiae Anglicanae Scriptores Decem* (1652).

[2] Corpus Christi College Cambridge 139: see Rollason, *LDE* p. xlii.

[3] Cambridge University Library Ff. i.27: see Rollason, *LDE* p. xlii.

[4] Durham University Library Cosin V.II.6 and British Library Cotton Faustina A.V: see Rollason, *LDE* p. xlii.

[5] Rollason, *LDE* pp. xlii–xliv; Arnold I pp. xx–xxiii; Gullick pp. 108–9; Symeon, *LDE* preface: Arnold I p. 1, Rollason, *LDE* pp. 2/3, Stevenson p. 624.

[6] Rollason, *LDE* pp. xxi note 22, xlv; Gullick pp. 93, 95, 97, 108–9; Symeon, *LDE* preface: Rollason, *LDE* pp. 8/9.

[7] Reginald xl: p. 84, Battiscombe p. 107, Raine, *Cuthbert* p. 86, Stevenson p. 780.

[8] Symeon, *LDE* preface: Rollason, *LDE* pp. 2/3, Arnold I p. 1, Stevenson p. 624.

[9] Rollason, *LDE* p. xlix.

[10] Rollason, *LDE* p. xlvi.

[11] Symeon, *LDE* iv 5: Rollason, *LDE* pp. 238/9, Arnold I p. 125, Stevenson p. 704.

[12] Turgot, *VSM* iv: Anderson II pp. 65–6.

[13] Turgot, *VSM* Introduction: Anderson II p. 59.

[14] Stevenson pp. vii–viii.

[15] Hutchinson II (1787, 1823) p. 66 note *.

[16] Hutchinson I p. 26.

[17] Hutchinson II (1787, 1823) p. 66 note *: *De exordio et progressu ecclesiae Dunelm ab anno 635 ad anno 1097*: BL MS Cotton Faustina A 5.

[18] Hutchinson II (1787, 1823) p. 66 note *.

[19] BL MS Cotton Tiberius D iii, dating from mid–13th century: Turgot, *VSM*: Anderson II pp. 59–88, Huneycutt App. II pp. 161–178, Hinde pp. 234–254. A later copy is in Madrid Biblioteca del Palacio Real MS II. 2097 fol. 26–41v.

[20] Turgot, *VSM* Introduction: Anderson II p. 59; Huneycutt p. 161.

[21] BL MS Cotton Tiberius E i: Turgot, *DSM*: Horstmann II pp. 168–175: "*vocato demum confessore suo Turgotus secundum priorem Dunelmiae, vita sua replicare coepit*". See also Horstmann I pp. ix–xiii; Huneycutt pp. 10–17, 161–2.

[22] Fordun: IV pp. 379, 376; Hinde pp. 255–266; Aelred, *Lament* 10: pp. 63–4; Aelred, *Genealogy* 20, 22 & 24: pp. 114, 116–7, 119–120.

[23] Hinde pp. lix–lx; Forster pp. 37–9.

[24] Forster pp. 38–9.

[25] Turgot, *VSM* xiii: Anderson II p. 84.

[26] Huneycutt p. 13.

[27] Colgrave p. 331.

[28] Bartlett p. 2.

7. Turgot, Friend of Scotland

[1] Symeon, *HR* s.a. 1070: Arnold II p. 192, Stevenson p. 553.

[2] Turgot, *VSM* ix: Anderson II p. 76.

[3] They met at Abernethy a few miles from the Norman ships: Douglas p. 227.

[4] Turgot, *VSM* iv: Anderson II p. 65: "*Ego ipse diutius ibidem*".

[5] Symeon, *HR* s.a. 1017: Arnold II p. 155, Stevenson p. 526; Aelred, *Genealogy* 19: p. 113; Ronay pp. 50–58, 184–5, citing Adam of Bremen ii 51 [p. 76], and *Leges Edwardi Confessoris Regis* s.35: David Wilkins, *Leges Anglo-Saxonicae ecclesiasticae et civiles* (London 1721) p. 208. [A shorter version of the *Leges* text reproduced in Ronay pp. 184–5 is printed in Thorpe p. 459.]

[6] Ronay pp. 109–121; Symeon, *HR* s.a. 1017: Arnold II p. 155, Stevenson p. 526; Florence, Appendix: Stevenson p. 402; *ASC* s.a. 1057: p. 184; *ASC* s.a. 1067: p. 198; Aelred, *Lament* 10: p. 63; Aelred, *Genealogy* 19: p. 113; Aelred, *Edward* 5: p. 141. Various alternative identifications are detailed in "Agatha, wife of Edward the Exile" on Wikipedia, the online encyclopedia (consulted 12.2010).

[7] Ronay pp. 102–8 citing Gaimar ii 4618–56 [p. 785].

[8] Turgot, *VSM* i: Anderson II p. 62. The personal name of Margaret spread from Italy in the eleventh century, when the parish church of Westminster, in the shadow of the abbey, was dedicated to St Margaret of Antioch.

[9] The title was conferred by Pope Alexander III on 7 February 1161. Edward's remains were translated by Becket on 13 October 1163 and Edward was revered as England's patron saint until 1222.

[10] Symeon, *HR* s.a. 1068: Arnold II p. 186, Stevenson p. 549. Aelred says they intended to return to Hungary—*Genealogy* 22: p. 116.

[11] Symeon, *HR* s.a. 1070: Arnold II p. 191, Stevenson p. 553.

[12] Aelred, *Genealogy* 20: p. 114.

[13] Fordun: IV pp. 379, 376; Hinde pp. 255–266; Aelred, *Lament* 10: pp. 63–4; Aelred, *Genealogy* 20, 22 & 24: pp. 114, 116–7, 119–120.

[14] Fordun v 15: IV p. 202, I p. 213.

[15] Aelred, *Lament* 10: pp. 63–4.

[16] Skene II p. 344; Moir Boyce p. 7.

[17] A similar cross was given by the queen to the church at St Andrews. See Turgot, *VSM* iv: Anderson II p. 65.

[18] Skene II p. 353 quoting Orderic Vitalis B viii c.22.

[19] Clover & Gibson no. 50 pp. 160–3.

[20] Lawrie no. 25 p. 21. It was finally founded by King David in 1128 and the buildings were completed and dedicated 1150: Wharton I p. 161.

[21] Turgot, *VSM* ix: Anderson II p. 75.

[22] Clover & Gibson no. 50 pp. 160–1.

[23] Turgot, *VSM* iv: Anderson II p. 65.

[24] Turgot, *VSM* vii: Anderson II p. 68.

[25] Turgot, *VSM* iv: Anderson II p. 66.

[26] Turgot, *VSM* vi: Anderson II p. 67.

[27] Turgot, *VSM* iii: Anderson II p. 64: "*gratiosa verborum facilitas*".

[28] Psalm 5:2: "*verba mea auribus percipe Domine*" "Listen to my words O Lord".

[29] *Liber Vitae* 52v3: II pp. 155–6; see also Barrow, *Kings* p. 314.

[30] *Durham Obitals*: p. 147.

[31] Skene II p. 353 quoting Orderic Vitalis B viii c.22.

[32] Turgot, *VSM* ix: Anderson II p. 77.

[33] Moir Bryce pp. 25–26. The chapel apse is circular internally and square externally, as were the presbytery apses at Durham.

[34] Turgot, *VSM* xii: Anderson II p. 81.

[35] Turgot, *VSM* xii: Anderson II p. 82.

[36] Turgot, *VSM* xii: Anderson II p. 82.

[37] Huneycutt pp. 17–18, 21–30, 147, citing: Eadmer: pp. 121–5; Hermann of Tournai, "Liber de restauratione S. Martini Tornacensis", in *Monumenta Germaniae Historica Scriptores* 14 (1956), pp. 281–2; Orderic Vitalis: Chibnall IV pp. 272/3; Walter Map, *De nugis curialem*: M. James (Oxford, 1983), p. 474; Matthew Paris, *Historia Anglorum*: F. Madden (London, 1866*) I pp. 188–9.

[38] Turgot, *VSM* xiii: Anderson II p. 83.

[39] Turgot, *VSM* xiii: Anderson II p. 84.

[40] Turgot, *VSM* xiii: Anderson II p. 85.

[41] Turgot, *VSM* xiii: Anderson II p. 85.

[42] Fordun v 21: IV p. 209, I pp. 219–20.

[43] *ASC* s.a. 1093: p. 230.

[44] Lawrie no. 15, p. 12; cf. no. 12 p. 10.

[45] Davis I no. 363 (cf. nos. 364–365 and notes to 363).

[46] Coldingham did not become a Benedictine monastery until about 1137, settled with Durham monks.

[47] Hutchinson I (1787) p. 139, (1823) p. 169.

[48] Forster p. 36 note.

[49] Fordun v 25: IV pp. 214–5, I pp. 224–5.

[50] *Liber Vitae* 15v5(1), 47r5(5): and see D.3 and III p. 16.

[51] Raine, *York* p. 363; Haddan & Stubbs II i pp. 159, 160.

[52] Bethell p. 34.

[53] Bethell pp. 33–45 citing Cambridge, Peterhouse, MS Peterhouse 74 fo. 218.

[54] Symeon, *HR* s.a. 1074: Arnold II p. 204, Stevenson p. 561; Knowles p. 170.

[55] Bethell p. 36.

[56] Green p. 17.

[57] Anderson II pp. 159–60 note 3.

[58] Fordun v 28: IV p. 218, I pp. 227–8. This became the first Augustinian house in Scotland.

[59] Symeon, *HR* s.a. 1074: Arnold II p. 205, Stevenson p. 561.

[60] Haddan & Stubbs II i p. 200.

[61] Entered on a leaf of the Register of St Andrews, which was written about 1130.

[62] Unlike early Scottish kings he was not buried at Iona, and may still lie at St Andrews.

[63] The Irish annals record the death of Tuathalan, abbot of Kilrimont, in 747.

[64] Haddan & Stubbs II i pp. 221–5.

[65] The relics consisted of a part of the arm, a knee-cap, three fingers of the right hand and a tooth.

[66] Anderson II pp. 205–6 note 5; Haddan & Stubbs II i pp. 225–7.

8. The Death of Turgot

[1] Symeon, *HR* s.a. 1074: Arnold II p. 205, Stevenson p. 561; Knowles p. 170.

[2] Symeon, *HR* s.a. 1074: Arnold II p. 205, Stevenson p. 561.

[3] le Neve: p. 172.

[4] Hugh the Chanter: p. 59.

[5] Symeon, *HR* s.a. 1074: Arnold II p. 205, Stevenson p. 562.

[6] Anderson, *Annals* p. 13 quoting Eadmer: p. 236; (cf. Hinde p. 97 note *t*).

[7] *Durham Obitals*: pp. 145, 151; (cf. Anderson, *Annals* p. 135; Anderson II p. 159 & note 2; Symeon, *HR* s.a. 1115: Arnold II p. 249, Stevenson p. 594).

[8] Symeon, *HR* s.a. 1074: Arnold II p. 205, Stevenson pp. 561–2.

[9] Symeon, *HR* s.a. 1074: Arnold II p. 205, Stevenson p. 562.

[10] Fowler, *Rites* p. 242.

[11] Turgot, *VSM* ii: Anderson II p. 63.

[12] British Library MS Harley 491.

[13] Harrison pp. 67–83. This article is the source of all information in this section, unless otherwise indicated. It appeared the year before publication of J. Dufour's five-volume study of mortuary rolls, *Recueil de Rouleaux des Morts (VIIIe siècle—1536)* (Académie des inscriptions et belles-lettres, 2005–2007), so some statements are probably in need of revision. Unfortunately, it has not been possible to access Dufour's work for the present study.

[14] Harrison p. 83, quoting D. Knowles (ed.), *The Monastic Constitutions of Lanfranc*, revised C. N. L. Brooke (Oxford, 2002) pp. 122–3.

[15] Symeon, *HR* s.a. 1074: Arnold II pp. 202–5, Stevenson pp. 560–3.

[16] Delisle no. xxxvi pp. 177–279.

[17] Maxwell pp. 36–7.

[18] Fowler, *Excavations* pp. 385–404.

[19] Hinde p. lxi.

[20] Symeon, *LDE* iv 8: Rollason, *LDE* pp. 242/3, Arnold I p. 128, Stevenson p. 706.

[21] Turgot, *VSM* ix: Anderson II p. 75.

Appendix: Turgot's *Life of St Margaret*

[1] This translation is taken from Anderson II pp. 59–88. The chapter headings have been incorporated into the text, rather than being left as a contents list as in the original. I am grateful to publisher Shaun Tyas for confirming that no changes were made to this translation in the 1991 reprint.

[2] 'Ironside'.

[3] Dunfermline.

[4] Ash Wednesday.

[5] Maundy Thursday.

[6] Psalm 51 in English versions.

[7] She died at Edinburgh and was buried at Dunfermline—see Fordun v 21: IV p. 209, I pp. 219–20.

Index

Lightning Source UK Ltd.
Milton Keynes UK
UKOW02f2317120417
299005UK00002B/96/P